Kings and Queens of India

Anu Kumar has studied history and management and, more recently, done a Master's in Fine Arts (Writing Fiction) from the Vermont College of Fine Arts, USA. She writes for readers of all ages. Her first fictional works for children were three books featuring Atisa, a young detective who travels through history on a specially designed balloon. Her books for children published by Hachette India include *The Mahatma and the Monkeys, Chanakya: The Kingmaker and the Philosopher, Sarojini Naidu: The Nightingale and the Freedom Fighter, Vivekananda: The Monk and the Reformer*, and twelve short books of the Myth Quest series.

KINGS AND QUEENS OF INDIA

Famous rulers and dynasties that shaped the country

ANU KUMAR

hachette
INDIA

First published in 2019 by Hachette India
(Registered name: Hachette Book Publishing India Pvt. Ltd)
An Hachette UK company
www.hachetteindia.com

SRD

Certain place names, such as Bombay, Calcutta, Mysore and Madras, among others, as well as the names of certain provinces and presidencies, such as Bengal and Madras, have been used to retain the historicity of the information, as far as possible with their new names.

ISBN 978-93-5009-947-6

Hachette Book Publishing India Pvt. Ltd
4th & 5th Floors, Corporate Centre
Plot No. 94, Sector 44, Gurugram - 122003, India

Typeset by Manmohan Kumar, Delhi

Printed and bound in India
by Manipal Technologies Limited, Manipal

CONTENTS

FIRST THINGS ABOUT
Rulers and Kingdoms

History seems to be defined by kings and queens, and many countries today continue to have them as heads of state. In the past, kings ruled over kingdoms, big and small; they fought wars and made laws for their subjects to follow. They wielded a lot of power, rewarding those who supported them, and woe betide anyone who became their enemy. For a long time, till checks and balances came in to restrain a ruler's power, they had the supreme right to punish their enemies.

In most cases, the rulers were usually men, and, hence, kings. Queens, as rulers, are far rarer in history. But even if most history books do not focus on them, it does not mean that queens had no important role other than being consorts. Most queens in royal families are recorded as awarding land grants to priests and scholars, and to religious centres. Many were patrons of art and literature.

There were also queens who wielded immense power and ruled on behalf of their husbands or minor children; a few even commanded armies.

Kings and queens, as we shall see, are just one way of studying history. It is a popular way since there are several historical sources on rulers. There are many texts and records, usually flattering, written by scholars and biographers. Many rulers minted their own coins and put up inscriptions detailing their achievements. By comparison, we don't have as much as information about common people and their lives in the past, though recent advances in archaeology have made it possible to find out more about them.

At the outset, we must remember that India of the past encompassed an area very different from today's political realities. Borders changed often, especially in the north-west and east, and in this book, India, especially ancient India, will include areas that now appear in present-day Afghanistan and Pakistan in the north-west, and Myanmar in the east.

The Birth of Kings and Queens

Kings and queens were a product of the times they lived in. Society (how people lived) and economy (what people did) were, in part, decided by geography – the turn of the land, the resources it provided, and the technological advancements of the time. In a major development, the development of the plough helped people move from a nomadic life to a settled life based on farming.

As agriculture became a vital economic activity, there was a greater need for regulated government and rules, such as who would cultivate the land, who would fight wars, and where the money would come for this. This is where rulers came in. In the beginning, they were 'chosen' by the people, and the strongest and bravest warrior, usually, was made the leader of his (rarely, her) people.

Our earliest evidence of kings and queens in India comes from the early Vedic Age (c. 1500–1000 BCE). Texts related to the time have helped to know about the Indo-Aryans, a group of people who spoke an Indo-European language.

However, much before the Indo-Aryans – more than 1,000 years before them – in around 3500–2000 BCE, the Harappan civilization, with its amazingly planned cities, spread across an area stretching from present-day north-eastern Afghanistan, through much of Pakistan, and into western and north-western India. The craft specialization (with trained artisans making different things), and the great difference in house types and sizes show that life was organized and trade was well regulated. This and the development of large-scale public works like granaries meant that political and administrative control was exercised over a wide area. But details about what the system of government or administration was and who headed it are largely a mystery, as the Harappan script remains to be deciphered.

The early Vedic texts mention that the chief of a tribe or clan in early societies was just one among equals. He was paid a share of the loot from war, and later, a share of the produce from agriculture in return for protection or leading the tribe in war. Then there were other groups, such as the priests who claimed to know the sacred rites and gave sanction to a chief's, and later to a king's, power. Kings needed support of these powerful religious and political groups that were often one and the same.

As people moved into more settled lives, social divisions emerged. According to historians of ancient India, the caste system based on social divisions was largely occupational. Yet, there was a lot of fluidity in most of Indian history. As we shall see, there were dynasties that seized power, became rulers, and *only then* gave themselves an impressive ancestry, or placed themselves higher on the caste ladder.

The Many Things Kings and Queens Did

Military power came to matter a great deal as this helped gain control over fertile regions. Agriculture after all was the largest source of income for kingdoms in early times. To coordinate and draw in surplus produce (what the farmers sold/exchanged) from villages around, and to manage land revenue for any state or society to be well-organized, helped the rise of urban centres or cities. Pataliputra, Kannauj, Madurai, Hampi, Delhi and other important capital cities were all urban centres that rose through Indian history, drawing in people, agricultural produce and commerce from areas around. Control over such places – cities and fertile plains – soon came to symbolize a king's power.

Wars were one way to establish this dominance. Kings, however, did not merely fight wars for war's sake. They led their kingdoms in war to ensure stability and order. A stable and secure administration meant a constant source of revenue. Gradually, trade became important as an economic activity. Some of the first gold coins were issued by dynasties such as the Kushans, as well as the Indo-Greeks before them, who became rich from trade as the caravans passed Central Asia towards China. The wealth of the southern kingdoms that drew rulers, like Alauddin Khilji in the 14th century, to try to conquer them came mainly from trade and their abundant mineral resources.

Kings and queens played an important role in encouraging economic activities. Some were also patrons of culture. Akbar, the Mughal emperor, commissioned translations of Sanskrit texts, including the Ramayana, into Persian. Krishnadevaraya of Vijayanagara, as another example, wrote poetry in Telugu, and his court drew scholars and poets from all over.

The king was usually 'consecrated' (formally recognized) after his succession with an elaborate ritual. Powerful Hindu kings and princes in ancient times performed important sacrifices, such as the Ashvamedha and the Rajasuya. Even in later dynasties, this kind of symbolism mattered, whether it was recognition and sanction granted by priests in ancient times, or as with the Delhi Sultanate in medieval India, a robe given by the Caliph of Baghdad, who was considered the political and spiritual head of Islamic communities.

The Road to Kingship

Kingship was usually but not always hereditary. This meant that the firstborn son did not always become king after the death of his father. Sometimes, the king would nominate a son he thought most capable of ruling. But most times, the other princes never accepted this, believing themselves to be equally suitable, if not more. Nobles threw in their support behind competing contenders for the throne, to reap benefits from it.

There was, indeed, much violence that came at the time of succession. This has been a common thread through Indian history. Ashoka, the Mauryan king, waged war with his siblings. In the south, the Chalukyas and the Cholas witnessed their own succession battles, and in the Delhi Sultanate and the Mughal Empire, wars of succession became brutal, and very costly as well, since support had to be won and nobles bribed on many an occasion. Political change was the only constant at this time.

Kingship could also be elective, though, as we move down the centuries, this became increasingly rare. As recently as the 8th century CE, Gopala was *elected* the king of Bengal, and he went on to establish the Pala dynasty. Sometimes the people made the selection, and at times it was the ministers who did so. In one of the folktales in the *Jatakas*, the courtiers of a king are believed to have asked the latter:

'When you are dead, my lord, to whom shall we give the white umbrella (symbol of kingship)?'

'Friends,' said the king, 'all my sons have a right to the white umbrella. But you may give it to him that pleases your mind.'

Kings and queens reflected and symbolized change in society. A change in dynasty, or rule of one family line, did not mean just a shift of rulers, but rather, it signified a wider change: an upheaval in society, a change in the influence of powerful groups, the dislocation of groups of people – that is, a time of chaos and churning and change.

This made for an interesting paradox: For a long time, economic change was, at best, gradual. Agriculture was what sustained people; trade and craft production were urban activities; and technological change was evident in weapons of war and in the ways, for example, sailing ships were designed. Yet political change was almost constant, as new dynasties supplanted older ones with regularity, and new groups of people came in from foreign lands, whether as invaders or as settlers. Their 'accommodation' meant that society was always in a state of flux, and that the caste system – for new groups of people had to be fitted within a hierarchy that decided marriage and eating rituals – was indeed fluid for a long time.

Dependable Shoulders and Wise Advisers

In ancient times, the king (or queen) was rarely ever a despot. The ruler's powers were checked; first, by priests, which was the scholarly community in those days; and second, by ministers and village headmen, whom the king consulted regularly. Another check, in the very ancient times, was supplied by the will of the people, who used to meet in an assembly-style *samiti* or *parishad* (committee). The ministers, or officials, were seen as the king's 'arms' – parts of the same being who had to work in perfect coordination.

Such 'democracies' ended once ruled areas grew larger in size and kingdoms were formed. But even though the king came to wield supreme power, he still had to rule as the benefactor of his people. This was not always so – the Nandas of the 3rd century BCE were known to have built large-scale irrigation projects, but their sheer greed, as recorded by the writers of the time, turned them into tyrants.

Rulers also needed a broad group of support, that is, people on whom the ruler could rely, especially since their extended family and the clan could be unreliable. Rulers like Amoghavarsha in the 9th century employed Arabs in administration, Krishnadevaraya of Vijayanagara had Portuguese gunners in the army, and Akbar reached out to the Rajputs. This was also essential in a region made up of varied people, following different beliefs and religions. Such a policy of reaching out and conciliation created better security for both the ruler and the ruled.

Queens – Behind the Scenes

Although their names don't feature as often as those of kings, queens did make their presence felt. From as early as the 1st century CE, their names have appeared on inscriptions. In the Deccan, the names of queens were inscribed on temples as the main benefactors. They also had the power to make certain decisions, to donate, and, in times of disputed succession, they could play a crucial role.

Moreover, matrimonial alliances – wherein a princess was married off to a rival king as a way of buying peace and alliance – led to a fusion of ideas and cultures, spearheaded chiefly by the new queen and her entourage. The queens wielded a lot of influence behind the scenes too, and were able to change policy on many an occasion. For instance, when Akbar's son Salim (later Emperor Jahangir) rebelled against his father, his grandmother Hamida Banu Begum and stepmother Salima Sultan interceded to ensure that Akbar forgave him.

Yet, there have been fewer queens as rulers in their own right than kings. One reason perhaps is that queens for a long time could not really lead armies into battle. There were stellar exceptions: Razia Sultan, Durgavati, and Lakshmibai, among others. Moreover, queens encountered all kinds of opposition – kings did too, of course, but there were many – scholars, conservative groups, and perhaps their own families too – who felt women could not really rule. To be a queen then meant one had to be not just extraordinary but also a bit of a rebel, someone who did things differently, like Razia who insisted on being called 'sultan'.

There has been a fascinating range of rulers throughout India's 2000-year history of kings and queens, or at least, since the time we have evidence about the country's rulers. They all, interestingly, had some things in common. Most of the rulers, especially kings, came to rule at a very young age. Chandragupta Maurya was apparently only 19 years old when he defeated the Nandas of Magadha around 323–322 BCE. Mughal Emperor Akbar was 13 when he lost his father and led his army into battle against Hemu. There are many more such examples. It's clear that if a king wanted to come to power and rule long and well, he had to be indeed exceptional in many ways; queens even more so!

BIMBISARA
The King Who Made Magadha

It may be hard to imagine now, but the area in and around present-day Bihar was once not only the home of the great ancient kingdom of Magadha, but also the birthplace of two of ancient India's most powerful empires – the Mauryan Empire and the Gupta Empire. What gave Magadha the extra edge was its strategic location. The richly forested and trade-heavy Ganga River valley formed its northern border, while the iron-yielding mountains of the Vindhya Range lay to its south. With these advantages, whoever ruled Magadha was in a position far superior to other kingdoms.

And it was a young prince, just 15 years old, who would set Magadha off on its route to greatness. In today's time, Bimbisara (reign: 543–491 BCE) would probably have been a class X student! But he was made king of Magadha by his father Bhattiya, the local chieftain. As per the custom

A ROYAL SECRET!

Buddhist texts credit Bimbisara with helping Siddhartha, before he became the Buddha, many a time. Later, the Buddha gave his sermons in the park called Veluvana, which Bimbisara had gifted him. One of his wives was said to be the Buddha's first female disciple.

of that area and time, other fellow chiefs, who were all equals, should have nominated Bhattiya's successor. But the chieftain's family was much more powerful than them, and Bimbisara became their ruler. Surrounded by several kingdoms that would, if given the slightest chance or sensing any weakness, snatch power, the teenage king had a long and difficult road ahead of him.

At this time, many small republics (lands ruled by a group of chiefs) lay spread around Magadha. These included the Lichchhavis of Vaishali, the Sakyas of Kapilavastu (the clan the Buddha belonged to!) and the Moriyas of Pipphalivana – all in the plains of the river Ganga and the Himalayan foothills. Some forest tribes and clans also had bases here. And if these weren't enough, three new kingdoms – Kosala, Vatsa, and Avanti – had emerged as threats. Realizing the peril around him, Bimbisara knew he had to strike first.

And strike he did. Strategically. There were two main tactics Bimbisara employed to protect his kingdom and gain territory. The first was through marriage alliances.

His first wife was Kosala Devi, the sister of Prasenajit, the powerful king of Kosala; Bimbisara gained the village of Kashi as part of the dowry, and the village brought with it the revenue to provide for the new queen's bath and perfume expenses! Now that's a sweet-smelling deal! His second wife was a Lichchhavi princess, the daughter of chief Chetaka of Vaishali. Through these and other similar alliances, Bimbisara gained not just additional land, but also strong allegiances against his enemies.

In cases where marriage was not possible or desirable, Bimbisara used military might to conquer smaller principalities. This included Anga, a formidable kingdom and long-time foe of Magadha. The young king captured Anga by killing its last king, Brahmadutta.

Slowly and steadily, Bimbisara established himself as a powerful ruler. His patronage of the Buddha helped the latter gain a big following. Bimbisara ruled for more than 50 years. In the end, it was not an outside enemy, but someone close to him who was the cause of his death in 491 BCE – his favourite son from his first wife, Ajatashatru.

WHAT AN IMPACT!

Bimbisara sensed Magadha's potential, and took advantage of its favourable position and access to resources to ensure its rise to power. He, as king, saw the 'big picture' – a vision of what Magadha could be, and its specific opportunities.

AJATASHATRU

An Impatient Prince, a Devious King

Ajatashatru, Prince of Magadha, (reign: 493/491–460 BCE), was the beloved son of King Bimbisara and Queen Kosala Devi. Little did his loving parents know, however, that this much-adored child would be the reason for his father's death!

Ajatashatru was named aptly. His name translates as one who would 'always be victorious over his enemies'. The young prince grew up to be brave. Unfortunately, he was also suspicious and scheming. Impatient to become king, Ajatashatru finally decided to take matters into his own hands. And one day, he seized control of the kingdom from Bimbisara, threw his aged father into prison and proclaimed himself king of Magadha.

According to another version, Ajatashatru did not imprison, but murdered his father (a crime known as patricide).

Ajatashatru goes to visit the Buddha

Soon after Bimbisara's imprisonment, Ajatashatru's mother narrated an old incident to her son. It was a tale that dated back to when Ajatashatru was a baby and was in danger of dying due to a poisonous bite on his finger. King Bimbisara had gathered the newborn in his arms and sucked the poison out from his forefinger, not stopping till the child was healed! Upon hearing this story the prince, now king, was overcome with remorse and rushed towards the prison to ask for his father's forgiveness. But Bimbisara heard him coming. Fearing his son's intentions, he killed himself.

After his father's death, a penitent Ajatashatru went to meet the Buddha to confess his sin and seek his blessings. The Buddha assured him that by confessing his crime and feeling remorse, he had become a better man and king.

This, however, was not to be. Ajatashatru's reign was even more aggressive than his father's. And he made no bones about it, using shrewd means to humble his enemies, even those related to him. This included Prasenajit, the Kosalan king and Ajatashatru's uncle, who was angered by Bimbisara's murder and the subsequent death of his sister, Ajatashatru's mother, who had died of grief. In addition to this, Ajatashatru had retained the revenues from the village of Kashi, which had been his mother's dowry on marriage.

Enraged with all this and by the new king's audacity, Prasenajit welcomed a battle with Ajatashatru. But it was no easy war. On one occasion, the Kosalan monarch was forced to flee in temporary defeat; in another contest, Ajatashatru found himself a prisoner of the Kosalan army.

But then, strangely, Prasenajit had a possible change of heart. Suspending conflict, he arranged a marriage alliance between his daughter and his captive nephew. All, however, was not to be well for long. A turbulent time still lay ahead of Kosala.

Some time after, while Prasenajit was away from his capital city, his own commander-in-chief, taking advantage of the king's absence, crowned Vidudabha, Prasenajit's son, as the new king of Kosala, in the hope that a younger king would be more pliable.

Ousted as king, Prasenajit immediately set out for Rajagriha, Magadha's capital, hoping to seek Ajatashatru's help in recapturing his kingdom. But the night was cold, and Prasenajit tragically died from exposure before reaching the city's gates. With Prasenajit gone, Ajatashatru needed little encouragement to declare war on Kosala once again. This time, he was successful. The kingdom of Kosala was now part of Magadha territory.

Ajatashatru then turned his attention to Vaishali, the seat of the powerful Lichchhavi clan. Situated north of the river Ganga (in an area now known Tirhut in present-

A ROYAL SECRET!

Ajatashatru is believed to have used two very innovative weapons (for the time) against the Vaishali army. The first was called *mahashilakantaka*, which seems to have been a giant catapult used to hurl large stones; the second was called *rathamusala*, a chariot with swinging maces on either side, which wreaked havoc as the chariot moved through the opposing forces.

day Bihar), this prosperous republic was a jewel worth possessing. Ajatashatru waged his campaign slowly and masterfully. The Buddha had advised the democratic Lichchhavis to hold periodic assemblies where its chief members would meet and take decisions collectively. As part of a devious plan, Ajatashatru sent his trusted minister to stealthily infiltrate this assembly. This disguised spy lived amongst the Lichchhavis for three years! Eventually, he won the trust of some of clan chiefs, and then, through rumour and gossip, turned them against each other.

The time was now ripe for an attack. As Ajatashatru prepared for war, Chetaka, chief of Vaishali, called on the other neighbouring kingdoms and republics to unite to fight an increasingly hostile common enemy – Magadha, that was now growing far too powerful.

What followed was one of ancient India's first recorded long wars. But in time, Magadha defeated the Lichchhavis and occupied Vaishali. The victors erected a fortress-city at the village of Patali on the bank of the river Ganga. Ajatashatru's son, Udayin, laid the foundations of this city, which went on to be known as Kusumapura, Pushpapura, or Pataliputra (now Patna). It soon grew in size and magnificence, and would go on to serve as the capital of future dynasties.

WHAT AN IMPACT!

Ajatashatru showed up yet another facet of kingship. A king had to be devious and ambitious in his bid for power. Though accused of heinous crimes, Ajatashatru made Magadha a very powerful kingdom and it would remain so for centuries to come.

PORUS
A Worthy Opponent

In the year 326 BCE, a legendary battle occurred on the banks of the river Jhelum. This was fought between two kings, Alexander, the Macedonian ruler, and Porus, who ruled in a region between the rivers Jhelum and Chenab in Punjab. We know of this battle from Greek sources: writers and chroniclers like Megasthenes and Arrian. The dates for Porus's reign are not very clear, given the scarcity of contemporary historical records, but it is estimated to have lasted from 326 BCE to 321 or 315 BCE.

In 326 BCE, as Alexander's forces advanced quickly, having conquered the regions of Gandhara (in present-day Afghanistan) and after kings further to the east, like Ambhi of Taxila, had submitted to him, Porus waited, refusing to bow down and ready to give battle. Their forces were almost equally matched. Besides, Alexander's forces were now helped by Ambhi and other rulers in that

Alexander's coin showing Porus on an elephant

region. Alexander's clever planning and Porus's heroic resistance and his dignified stance after his defeat are now the stuff of folklore. The battle, in turn, has added to the mythical quality that Porus has acquired over the centuries.

Historical sources now conjecture that Porus was head of an early Vedic tribe (in around 1500 BCE) called the Purus. There is also a theory that he was part of the Shurasenas, a tribe that traced its origin to the god Krishna.

By the time Alexander and his forces arrived by the river Jhelum, across which lay Porus's kingdom, it was summer. The river was in spate, thanks to the snow melting in the high Himalayas. This made Alexander's soldiers, already restless from their long journey away from home, even more nervous. Yet Alexander was keen to advance further, for he had heard much about the fabled wealth of the Indian subcontinent.

Porus's army, fifty thousand strong, was already drawn up on the opposite bank. Alexander made his plans carefully. He distracted the enemy by giving the impression that an attack was imminent; yet all the time he had his men prepare a makeshift bridge a bit upriver by placing logs across it. One night when the rain fell unexpectedly heavily, he led his men and they forded the river quietly and swiftly. In this manner, Alexander managed to take the enemy by surprise.

A ROYAL SECRET!

The legend of Porus has been commemorated in films and on television. Actors like Sohrab Modi and Prithviraj Kapoor played Porus in films made in 1941 (*Sikandar*) and 1965 (*Sikandar-e-Azam*) respectively. Since then, Porus has been a staple feature in all films, television serials and animated series based on Alexander or even Chandragupta Maurya.

As the story goes, the elephants in Porus's army panicked and bolted. It was also too late by the time a message for help reached Porus's son, who came up to offer battle, leading a cavalry of 2,000 horsemen and others on their chariots. But taken by surprise, this huge but poorly prepared force was speedily routed.

Porus, described by writers of the time as a magnificent giant of a man, six and a half feet in height, fought to the end, but at last was taken prisoner. Alexander had the generosity to respect his brave opponent, and responded to his request to be 'treated as a king'. The victor not only returned to Porus his territory, but added to it other lands. Thus, Alexander secured a grateful ally for the remainder of his stay in the country.

Alexander's armies, despite their victory over Porus, did not want to continue onward to the plains. In fact, Alexander was threatened with open rebellion. Some months later, a disappointed Alexander gave in to the demand of his troops to return home. However, Alexander himself would never make it home. He died at Babylon in Egypt in 323 BCE, at the age of thirty-three.

There is considerable uncertainty over how Porus died. He was apparently killed by one of Alexander's generals, Eudemus, as Alexander's 'satraps' (provincial governors) fought each other to gain control over the area he had conquered. In one version, as the play *Mudrarakshasa* written several centuries later has it, Porus was apparently poisoned to death. Barely some years later, Chandragupta of the Mauryas would conquer this region on his way to building up ancient India's largest empire.

WHAT AN IMPACT!

The defeat of the kings of this region, including Porus's, made it somewhat easier for Chandragupta to assert his authority some years later. There was chaos and uncertainty as Alexander's satraps and the smaller kings were now considerably weakened, and Chandragupta, a skillful general and warrior, quickly established Mauryan hold over these parts.

CHANDRAGUPTA MAURYA
The End of Tyranny

Almost 150 years after Ajatashatru, Magadha would see the rise of one of ancient India's greatest rulers. Chandragupta Maurya (reign: 321–297 BCE), set up an empire that stretched far beyond Magadha's borders, to include areas in present-day Afghanistan and those as far south as the rivers Krishna and Godavari. He was 19 years old at the time he became king of Magadha.

The story of Chandragupta's ascension to the Magadha throne is one of triumph, but with several twists and turns.

Following Ajatashatru's death, Magadha's own story turned somewhat tragic. Some texts narrate that most of the kings who succeeded Ajatashatru were guilty of parricide. Eventually, the people rebelled against their ruler and banished Naga Dasaka, the last king of Ajatashatru's dynasty. They replaced him with a minister named Sisunaga, then based at Benares (present-day Varanasi in

Uttar Pradesh). But this dynasty did not last long either and was, in turn, overthrown by the line of the Nandas.

The Nanda dynasty was feared. Its founder, Mahapadma, and his nine sons were known to be tyrants. They overtaxed farmers and merchants, while themselves living in luxury and maintaining an immense army. Around the end of the 4th century BCE, when Mahapadma's son, Dhana Nanda, ruled Magadha, the armies of Alexander, the mighty ruler of the ancient Greek kingdom of Macedonia, appeared in the north-west, close to the river Indus and its tributaries. As Alexander's army set up camp, many of his soldiers and commanders heard about the size of the Nanda army and the large number of elephants they possessed. (Evidently, gossip travelled fast even in ancient times!) Made uneasy and fearful by these rumours, Alexander's army refused to move against the Nandas. Unable to persuade them to change their minds, Alexander was forced to abandon his plans and decided to return to his homeland.

The year was 325 BCE. It may have seemed to the Nandas that they had just escaped a huge threat. What they didn't realize then, however, was that the real danger to their rule would come within a few years from someone they would have thought insignificant: from Chandragupta Maurya, then a young man on the run.

Little is known with certainty about Chandragupta's origins. Some sources, written several years after his time, state that he was not of noble origin, and was known as Moriya to the locals before he became a ruler; Greek accounts refer to him as Sandrokottos. One story suggests he was the son of a Nanda prince with a lower-caste (or slave, as another story has it) woman. Yet other texts believe he belonged to the Moriya clan, which had been oppressed by the Nandas, and who lived in the Himalayan foothills, in a region called Pipphalivana. Another story proposes that the Nandas considered him to be a threat from quite early on. And Chandragupta was forced to escape from Magadha, fearing for his life, spending subsequent years on the run, while plotting his revenge against the Nandas.

This period on the run gave rise to many stories of Chandragupta's daring exploits and encounters. According to one, once, when Chandragupta was asleep, a lion came up to him and licked off the young boy's sweat. In another story, Chandragupta single-handedly tamed a wild elephant into submission.

Chandragupta, apparently, also visited Alexander when the Macedonian king was camping in the Indian north-west. It was his intention to persuade the conqueror to put an end to the rule of the tyrant of Magadha. But Chandragupta found Alexander to be as great a tyrant as Dhana Nanda. Alexander, in turn, was offended by his bold speech, and gave orders to kill him. But Chandragupta escaped just in time.

Eventually, Chandragupta formed an army from scratch by enlisting a band of men drawn from robbers, fugitive soldiers and others, to challenge the Nandas. It is during this time that he is believed to have conquered Punjab (although this is debated) and added to his army. His childhood mentor and guru, who grew to be the political strategist and 'kingmaker' Chanakya (or Kautilya), a man with origins as mysterious as Chandragupta's, helped and advised him during this process. It is possible that Chandragupta also made use of the many soldiers who left Alexander's service when the Greeks prepared to leave India. It was with this ragtag army, that Chandragupta advanced on the Nandas.

Around 323–322 BCE, Chandragupta marched on to Magadha. Hearing the news of the arrival of his determined force, Dhana Nanda's soldiers deserted in droves, and Dhana Nanda, as the story goes, fled just moments before, taking part of his great treasure with him.

Chandragupta's success and accession appeared to be almost a miracle. His victory made it even more clear that the Nandas were hugely unpopular. After all, they were defeated not by a powerful ruler but by a nobody of uncertain lineage.

Conquering Punjab and Magadha was not Chandragupta's only achievement. As ruler and commander of an immense army, Chandragupta also crushed the satraps or generals appointed by Alexander to oversee the Greek conquests in India. One of Chandragupta's most famous campaigns was against Seleucus Nikator, a former Macedonian general of Alexander. After Alexander's death, Seleucus had taken over much of Alexander's empire in west Asia. He then wanted to make an expedition into India, and crossed the river Indus to challenge Chandragupta for control of north India. A battle raged between the two great warriors.

In the end, Seleucus opted to make peace with Chandragupta and married off his daughter to Chandragupta. In their treaty of peace, Chandragupta presented 500 elephants to Seleucus, who, in turn, conceded some of the lands situated along the river Indus – the four regions of Afghanistan called Aria (present-day Herat), Arachosia (Kandahar), Gedrosia (the area around Baluchistan) and Paropamisadai (Kabul) – to the Magadhan emperor.

Chandragupta had now extended his empire into western Asia, much beyond the river Indus. But the young king's realm was still expanding. Certain inscriptions in Mysuru, Karnataka, refer to Chandragupta's rule in north Mysuru, which means that Mauryan rule extended deep into southern India too. He also pushed his conquests as far as Saurashtra in western India. An inscription in this region, placed 200 years later by Saka ruler Rudradaman refers to Pushyagupta, Chandragupta's viceroy, who constructed the famous Sudarshana Lake on the emperor's instructions. Yes, Chandragupta Maurya was now Emperor of India.

Once Chandragupta had secured power, he was wise enough to follow the very wise advice of his mentor Chanakya, who wrote the *Arthashastra* – a powerful treatise on political and military strategies for a strong and enduring rule. His first step was to consolidate his base by setting up a sound administration, with checks and balances on every branch of government, and an extensive, well-equipped and diverse army, with soldiers from all over joining together to serve the Mauryan cause.

Much of the information about the Mauryan rule comes from Megasthenes, a friendly envoy sent to the Mauryan court by Seleucus. His writings were preserved in later texts. He and Chanakya have also left detailed accounts of Chandragupta's government, and the later edicts of his grandson, the great King Ashoka, confirm how the Mauryan Empire was governed.

The Mauryan government under Chandragupta consisted of two main parts: the raja (king) and the bureaucracy led by a council of ministers made up of *mahamatras* (governors), *amatyas* (senior civil officials), and *sachivas* (officials). The raja was the head of the state, and had the final say on all things – military, judicial and even routine administration.

The *mahamatras* and *amatyas* advised the king on all matters. Among the *sachivas* and *amatyas*, the most important were the *mantrins* or high ministers. They were appointed after their character had been tested against every possible temptation, so as to guard against corruption, disloyalty and unfairness. They were given the highest salary: 48,000 *panas* every year (the Mauryans issued punch-marked coins, usually of silver, of various weights). The *mantrins* assisted the king in employing other *amatyas* and attended royal functions associated with the reception of envoys.

They even accompanied the king to the battlefield. Chanakya was also a *mantrin* – the most important one of all. In matters of emergency – if war had to be waged, for example – they were summoned along with the *mantriparishad* (assembly of imperial councillors) to counsel the king. In theory, the king had to listen to the verdict of the majority in the assembly. In reality, however, it appears that the king's decision was generally accepted.

Other *amatyas* were employed in civil and criminal courts. Some were appointed to supervise the 'pleasure houses' set up to entertain merchants and foreign dignitaries (this actually was a way of keeping an eye on them), while others were employed in mines as well as forests for timber, and elephants.

There was even a class of men called overseers (spies) who kept an eye on most things done all through the kingdom and gave their reports to the king or his deputies.

The *adhyakshas* or the magistrates were in charge of different things, such as the market, how the cities were managed and how the soldiers were organized. Some administered the land and the revenue. Others oversaw the roads and the craftsmen while still others managed the public services that made an empire efficient.

The *Arthashastra* in fact laid down principles for *every* aspect of state policy, ranging from diplomacy and foreign relations, to how the army was to be organized, the upkeep of elephants, and a list of detailed punishments for every kind of crime. An interesting fact is that Mauryan officials

A ROYAL SECRET!

To guard against enemies, Chanakya who was Chandragupta's adviser, planned against every possibility. Sometimes, it is said, he would add little amounts of poison to Chandragupta's food to make him, gradually immune to it. But tragedy struck when Chandragupta's wife, Durdhara, who was then expecting a child, took in a small amount of poison in food meant for Chandragupta. She died soon after. And as the story goes, it was Chanakya's quick intervention that saved the young prince Bindusara's life.

at the time were paid salaries, like regular office goers! They did not receive a grant of land in lieu of salaries as would be done later in subsequent dynasties.

It is hard to imagine, but after achieving so much success and power, Chandragupta yet again proved his uniqueness by renouncing everything and becoming a Jain monk. One day, Bhadrabahu, the king's spiritual guru, prophesied that a 12-year long famine was on its way. Chandragupta decided to give up his throne and follow his beloved guru to south India. And so, after a reign of 24 glorious years, he crowned his son, Bindusara, and left his kingdom, never to look back.

It is believed that he walked all the way to Mysuru! Two inscriptions, dated to around 900 CE, on the bank of the river Kaveri near Srirangapatna, mention that the footprints of Chandragupta and Bhadrabahu can be seen on the summit of the Chandragiri Hill. It is here that both guru and disciple began a fast till death as part of a Jain ritual. In 297 BCE, Chandragupta Maurya died.

Chandragupta's son, Bindusara Amitraghata (the latter name means 'slayer of foes') was the second Mauryan emperor. Chanakya continued to be part of Bindusara's administration and the empire remained as vast as before. His rule was long and largely peaceful, although one notable town in the north-west Taxila, revolted during his reign. The king sent his most capable son, Ashoka, to restore order. As the prince neared Taxila with his troops, the people came out to meet him and complained about the city's officials. This would later compel Ashoka, when he was king, to institute a system of regular transfers of his officials, just so that they would not oppress the people.

WHAT AN IMPACT!

Chandragupta ruled with certain precepts and principles in mind, and he was assisted by officials and bureaucrats who followed rules and policies. In a short span of time, he built up a powerful and big empire. He was also unique in being a king who chose to give up his kingdom to live out his last days as a monk.

ASHOKA
The King Who Chose Peace

Ashoka (reign: 268–232 BCE) succeeded Bindusara to become the third emperor of the mighty Mauryan Empire. However, it wasn't an easy succession. He first had to wage a violent war against his stepbrothers, several of whom were killed in the battle for the throne. Eventually, Ashoka triumphed over everyone.

In every measure, Ashoka would prove himself worthy of being Chandragupta's grandson. And like his grandfather, he would show his uniqueness by becoming a king who would, one day, actively give up war and speak up for *dhamma* or dharma. But for a long time, the entire story of who Ashoka was and what he really did remained one of history's long unresolved mysteries.

This is how the mystery unravelled. Many old Buddhist texts refer to a king called Devanam Piyadassi (Beloved of the Gods). This name was also found inscribed on several old pillars and edicts found across north and north-western India; these pillars talk of rules related to *dhamma* – a code for moral living and good conduct. No one knew who this king was. The puzzle surrounding the identity of Devanam Piyadassi was finally decoded in the late 19th century, by a group of scholars known as Orientalists, comprising British officials and their Indian associates.

James Prinsep, an official of the British East India Company, played a leading role in interpreting these edicts. He learnt the Brahmi script (used for the ancient inscriptions) with the help of local officials, and found a repeated reference to a king called Piyadassi on the edicts. Prinsep had no idea who this Piyadassi was. But clarification came soon enough when George Turnour, a civil servant in Ceylon (Sri Lanka) identified the king as Ashoka on the basis of references in an ancient Buddhist book called the *Mahavamsa*, written in the Pali script. The book was about ancient kings and here, both names, Ashoka and Piyadassi, were mentioned together.

Several years later in 1915, C. Beadon, a British gold-mining engineer in Mysuru, Karnataka, found an inscription in a village called Maski (in Raichur district, Karnataka) that confirmed that the king Piyadassi was, in fact, Ashoka. Yet another inscription found in the village of Gujarra, in the Datia district of Madhya Pradesh, features Ashoka's name along with Devanam Piyadassi.

The road to power is rarely smooth. And so it was with Ashoka. Old Buddhist texts talk of a fiery struggle between the Mauryan princes after the death of King Bindusara in 272 BCE. Known for his terrible temper and cruelty, Ashoka overthrew his eldest stepbrother, the heir apparent, with the help of Radhagupta, a loyal minister whom Ashoka later made his chief minister upon ascending the throne. His formal coronation (*abhisheka*), however, took place a few years later in 268 BCE, which perhaps confirms the truth about the struggle among the princes.

Soon after becoming king, Ashoka suppressed a revolt of Taxila, a region that seemed to be in a perpetual state of unrest. After all this violence, it was in the thirteenth year of his reign that Ashoka marched into war with Kalinga (a large part of present-day Odisha and northern Andhra Pradesh), to wage a battle that texts of the period and later would record as one of the bloodiest ever fought. According to Buddhist texts: 'One hundred and fifty thousand persons were carried away captive, one hundred thousand were slain, and many times that number died.' The sight filled Ashoka with great remorse and he finally understood the need for peace. This drew him towards Buddhism and its message of non-violence.

The idea of installing rock inscriptions and erecting pillars to spread his message of peace and goodwill may have come to Ashoka on hearing about the rock inscription set up in Persepolis (Iran) by King Darius of Persia. Interestingly, Ashoka's edicts and inscriptions mainly reflect his duties as an emperor; only in some do they show his personal beliefs as a Buddhist. These inscriptions explain in detail what is known as Ashoka's *dhamma* or dharma in Sanskrit, which means 'universal law or righteousness' (living life in a morally upright way).

Ashoka's *dhamma* was meant for all his subjects; no matter what religion they followed. It stressed good conduct and social responsibility, that is, the need to be kind and well disposed toward all beings. His *dhamma* emphasized non-violence. But Ashoka was still the emperor of a vast kingdom, and he had to be practical too. He said he would not wage war and advised his successors not to do so either.

However, where conquest was essential and couldn't be avoided, he insisted that it had to be done keeping all practical considerations in mind. For example, in one edict found in Kalinga, the emperor made it known that people residing on the frontiers of his empire (other kingdoms beyond the Mauryan border) should not be afraid of Magadha, and that they should trust its rulers. And so, true to principle, Ashoka made no attempt to annex the frontier kingdoms (though, of course, it was clear that such kingdoms were too small and weak to ever pose a threat to the Magadhan emperor). Ashoka also gave these kings advice (perhaps unsolicited) on occasion, and established charitable institutions in their dominions. Ashoka maintained friendly relations not only with the powers to the south, but also with rulers of kingdoms farther away, such as in western Asia, Egypt and Macedonia.

Ashoka reached out to other kings – for instance, the King of Ceylon (Sri Lanka) – as a promoter of Buddhism, too. In fact, his son, Mahendra, and daughter, Sanghamitra, travelled to Anuradhapura (Ceylon's capital) to explain the precepts and practices of Buddhism to the people there. Similar missions were sent to Suvarnabhumi (now in Myanmar) too.

In Magadha, Ashoka appointed new officials known as *dharmamahamatras* and *dharmayutas*. It was their duty to publicize the emperor's message of *dhamma* among the people. They travelled far and wide, to provinces beyond Magadha, such as Kalinga, Ujjayini and Taxila.

At that time, river valleys and roads were the chief travel routes within India. While the distances were long, it helped that the condition of roads during the Mauryan period was much improved. Lucky Mauryans! Greek sources talk of a royal highway built by the Mauryas, connecting Taxila with Pataliputra and terminating at Tamralipti, the main port in the Ganges delta: the Grand Trunk Road, as it would be called, of the future.

On the western coast, the port of Bhrigukachchha (modern Bharuch) was linked to the Ganga plains via Rajasthan and Ujjain. From the Narmada Valley, there were routes going toward the Deccan and continuing along rivers flowing eastward towards south India.

While his officers were busy preaching the new order, the emperor wasn't idle. Ashoka visited Bodh Gaya, a holy place associated with Buddhism, and set out on tours of piety (*dhammayata*). Such tours included visiting ascetics and monks of all sects, and making generous donations to

A ROYAL SECRET!

The Lion Capital, with four lions standing back to back, that once stood atop Ashoka's Sarnath pillar near Varanasi in present-day Uttar Pradesh is today India's national emblem. What's more, the chariot wheel at the base of the capital appears at the centre of India's national flag.

them. It also included visiting people all across his empire, and instructing them in ways of the *dhamma*. Ashoka was both a father figure and a preacher king!

Ashoka abolished the sacrificial slaughter of animals, especially the regular killing of animals in the royal kitchen. He established hospitals for both people and animals. All along the roads, wells were dug and trees planted for the comfort of travellers, man and beast. As records show, more than 700 years later, in the 5th century CE, the rest houses and free hospitals of Magadha won the admiration of foreign travellers such as Fa-hsien (Faxian) and Xuanzang.

Just as Ashoka wanted friendship and harmony between the various sects in his empire, he wanted to prevent divisions within the Buddhist church too. He convened a Buddhist Council in Pataliputra and asked them to collect and prepare a unified sacred text for Buddhism.

Ashoka ruled for 36 years, and it is clear that his empire was indeed vast, especially given that his edicts have been found far afield, including the north-west of the Indian subcontinent. However, it did not survive long after his death in 232 BCE. The reasons are not difficult to see. A massive state apparatus, with many officials, some appointed to spread the cause of *dhamma*, had to be maintained at a huge cost. and this created a strain on resources. But while trade had expanded, the resources from it and the agrarian produce were just not enough to sustain so many officials. Also, it was difficult to expect governors sitting in far-flung corners to remain loyal to a king. Eventually, Ashoka's successors could not hold the sweeping empire together, and it splintered.

WHAT AN IMPACT!

In his advocacy of 'dhamma', Ashoka believed it wasn't enough to be a conqueror of people and rule by fear. As king, Ashoka believed he should be benevolent, and be a kind of 'father figure' to his people, telling them how to be good human beings and live good lives.

ROYAL GALLERY

Kalinga's Kharavela

In the 1st century CE, Kalinga emerged as a strong state in the east. One of its most famous rulers was Kharavela. His regnal dates are uncertain and historians believe he lived and ruled in the 2nd or 1st centuries BCE. More is known about him from his rock-cut Hathigumpha inscription (in present-day Udayagiri, Odisha). He was a patron and follower of Jainism, and a powerful military conqueror as well. According to his inscriptions, Kharavela defeated the kings of western Deccan and the north-west. He also humbled the Pandyan kingdom in the south – it is believed he had their fields ploughed by an ass, a gesture that indicates contempt. He also continued the irrigation works of the Nandas in his kingdom, and held many festive gatherings in his city.

Menander: The King Who Asked Many Questions

After the end of the Mauryan dynasty came the Shungas, and then several new kingdoms emerged in east

India. Meanwhile, the political situation in west and north-west India proved very volatile as the Khyber Pass was now unguarded.

The Indo-Greek rulers of Bactria and Iranian rulers of Parthia (present-day parts of Afghanistan and Iran) broke away from Seleucid rule (the dynasty of Alexander's general, Seleucus Nikator) in mid-3rd century BCE. The Indo-Greeks, as historians suggest, were actually an 'amalgam' of various ethnic groups, including those from east Europe, who might have descended from Alexander's armies. Indo-Greek rulers also had links to Scythian and Bactrian groups in west and Central Asia.

By the 2nd century BCE, the Indo-Greeks under their king Demetrius had moved east from Persia–Afghanistan, and entered Punjab. They gained control of north-western India (this included parts of present-day Pakistan). We know of these kings largely from their coins. Indo-Greek coins were the first to feature engraved portraits of the rulers, as well as legends inscribed in Greek, Brahmi and Kharosthi scripts – common in these parts.

The best-known among all the Indo-Greek kings was Menander, who ruled over a vast portion of north-west India – from Gandhara (in present-day Afghanistan), the Swat Valley (in Pakistan), the Hazara district in Punjab, and as far east as the river Ravi during 155–130 BCE. Interestingly, he was a devoted follower of Buddhism, and even appears in their texts where he is referred to as

Milinda. The Buddhist text *Milinda-Panha* (Questions of Milinda) is written in the form of a conversation between the king and the Buddhist philosopher Nagasena, wherein Menander is persuaded to adopt Buddhism.

Three Dynasties in the South

From the 2nd century BCE to the early years of the 1st millennium CE, three major chiefdoms – they really cannot be called kingdoms – existed in Tamilakam (abode of the Tamils, as the region was called then): the Pandya dynasty in Madurai (south and east Tamil Nadu); the Cheras on the Malabar Coast and its interior (modern-day Kerala), and the Cholas who dominated the area around Thanjavur and the Kaveri Valley (northern Tamil Nadu).

This period in the south was called the Sangam Age – a time when literary masterpieces were composed. The best-known of these are the epic poems, *Silappathikaram* and *Manimegalai*. The author of the first, Ilango Adigal, was a prince and a patron of Buddhism. The central figure of the first epic is Kannagi, a woman whose valour and revenge leads to a curse on the city of Madurai. Then follows her transformation to the Goddess Pattini. The latter is a sequel written by Chithalai Satthanar, who came from a merchant family.

GAUTAMIPUTRA SATAKARNI
Winner of Great Wars

Three centuries or so after Ashoka, around the first century CE, Gautamiputra Satakarni emerged as the first important Satavahana king – not in Magadha, but in the Deccan, in parts now known as east and north Maharashtra, Andhra Pradesh, Telangana and north Karnataka. The capital city of his dynasty was at Pratisthana (Paithan) in present-day Maharashtra.

The Satavahana rulers – and Gautamiputra first began this trend – were named after their mothers, stressing the important role women had in the dynasty. The Satavahanas were also called Andhras, probably because they resided in eastern Deccan (the Andhra region). In any case, their rule lasted around four centuries, from 1st century BCE to the 3rd century CE.

A dedicated warrior, Gautamiputra waged a series of successful wars against his many rivals. This included his

Coin featuring Gautamiputra Satakarni

north-western neighbours, especially the Sakas. In fact, the Saka–Satavahana wars make up one of the longest-running conflicts in ancient Indian history. He also waged war against the Pahlavas, and other *yavanas* (foreigners) who had appeared in Malwa (north-western Madhya Pradesh) and Kathiawar (west Gujarat).

Gautamiputra's feud against the Sakas continued for generations after his death, despite peace treaties and a marriage alliance. The two dynasties first came into conflict when the Sakas, who occupied parts of north India, were 'pushed' there and then forced to move further south by the Chinese emperor Shi Huang Ti, who began building the Great Wall of China to keep invaders out. As a result, the Sakas were engaged in battle with the Satavahanas, who ruled over many parts of this region.

When Gautamiputra won his first major battle against the Sakas – defeating the chief Nahapana – his mother issued an inscription (that bears her name) in 144 CE, praising her son for his victory.

The Satavahanas now extended their reach into north Deccan, and even acquired trading ports such as Bharuch in the west. The older Saka coins issued in this region were overstruck with the name Gautamiputra Satakarni as a sign of his victory. Defeated, the Sakas agreed to pay tribute and even served under the Satavahanas. The local government

A ROYAL SECRET!

One port town the Satavahanas and Sakas fought over was Bhrigukachchha (present-day Bharuch). Located in Kathiawar in southwestern Gujarat, it was called Barygaza in Roman records, a word that means 'deep treasure'. Lots of Roman gold coins, most of them belonging to the Roman emperors Augustus and Tiberius, have been found at Bhrigukachchha, so the name given it by the Romans was well deserved!

of the western provinces (Saurashtra) was entrusted to Chashtana, a Saka, but who was now the viceroy (satrap) to the Andhra conqueror.

Soon, the Saka king Rudradaman, grandson of viceroy Chashtana, would claim these regions. Things began to go downhill shortly after 138 CE, when Vasishthiputra Pulumavi, Gautamiputra's son, ascended the throne. Rudradaman resumed the Sakas' bid for their independent kingdom. The battle between the Sakas and Satavahanas was so intense that in order to end the bitter rivalry, the Satavahana king, Vasishthiputra, was married to Rudradaman's daughter, Dakshamitra. But this relationship did not stop Rudradaman, an ambitious and energetic ruler, from declaring war on his son-in-law.

This time, the Saka satrap was victorious. However, the victor Rudradaman contented himself with acquiring some Satavahana territory – and so, Saurashtra, Malwa and parts of the Konkan (west coast of India) passed to the Saka satraps.

The last of the important Satavahana kings was Yajnashri Satakarni, who ruled at the end of the 2nd century CE. He managed to assert Satavahana authority over the Sakas. The silver coins he issued were perhaps struck for circulation in areas he had re-conquered. Some of these feature the figure of a ship and this suggests that trade played an important role in these times.

Between around 200 BC and 200 CE, the *yavanas* came, bringing in fine lamps, gold and wine. In return, they bought huge amounts of pepper at the ports of south and west India. Purchases from India also included luxury articles – jewels, textiles, and animals for entertainment (apes, parrots and peacocks) – for wealthy Romans.

WHAT AN IMPACT!

As evident from land records and inscriptions, the Satavahana queens were held in high regard and wielded a lot of power. It was the first time queens appeared as donors and in their son's names, and not as mere consorts.

KANISHKA
A Warrior and a Buddhist

Like the Sakas, the Yueh-Chis were a nomadic group from Central Asia, who were forced to move south towards India. This was because their herds – of cattle and horses – needed grazing grounds, and the powerful Han empire in China posed a great threat. The Kushans were one of the groups that made up the Yueh-Chis, and they established their rule over a large part of north India and areas now in Afghanistan and Pakistan. One of the most celebrated Kushan kings was the fourth ruler of the dynasty, Kanishka (reign: 127–140/150 CE).

Kushan inscriptions, however, state that he ascended the throne in 78 CE. This year marks the beginning of the Saka era, and defines the Hindu calendar to this day. It was a calendar that Kanishka founded himself. The inscription lists his predecessors, and this too is quite remarkable for its time. Kanishka, like kings of that time and after, gave himself a: illustrious lineage!

Coin depicting Kanishka

Ancient texts record the exchanges and even the rivalries between the Yueh-Chis and the Chinese empire. As one story goes, one of the Kushan kings – Kanishka's predecessor – had rashly ventured into battle against the Chinese emperor. Under the leadership of the celebrated diplomat and general, Ban Chao, the Chinese army had embarked on a series of victories as they marched westward, reaching as far as the borders of the Roman Empire in west Asia.

As the story cited in the ancient Chinese texts goes, the Kushan king wished to assert a relationship of equality with the Chinese emperor, since the former had assisted the Chinese on several campaigns with the tribes to the west (in Central Asia). And so he asked for the hand of a Chinese princess in marriage. Ban Chao not only refused the proposal, but also arrested the Kushan envoy carrying the request. Greatly insulted, the Kushans put together a formidable force and sent it across the Pamir Mountains (in present-day Tajikistan in Central Asia) to attack the Chinese. The army, however, was unable to bear the severe cold and privations of this long march, and when it emerged into the plains of China in the north, it fell prey to Ban Chao's much smaller army and was defeated.

The Kushans were compelled to pay tribute to China, and Chinese texts mention the arrival of several tribute-bearing missions – usually carrying an abundance of gold, silks and items made of ivory.

When Kanishka came to the throne, he chose a wise and more sensible course. Not wishing to draw China's ire, he instead first focused on extending the Kushan dominions toward the south and east. And so he conquered Kashmir, where he built many monuments and monasteries in the valley, and founded a town, Kanishkapur, as well. He then led his army in an attack eastward, towards Mathura. After this conquest, it is said that he 'carried off' the famous and deeply respected Buddhist monk Ashvaghosha in one of his raids; from then on, the great Buddhist teacher graced Kanishka's court.

Kanishka's most striking military exploit, however, was his conquest of Kashgar, Yarkand and Khotan – all provinces to the north of Tibet. At that time, these were controlled by China. Through this region ran the famous Silk Road, all the way to west Asia. Thereafter, Indian merchants soon established trading stations here. This was a prosperous time indeed as seen in the gold coins issued during Kushan times.

Kanishka then took on the might of the Chinese and succeeded in freeing himself from the obligation of paying tribute to China. The story goes that he defeated the Han emperor's allies in Central Asia and compelled the defeated kings to give over hostages, including a son of the Han emperor, who was present in this region – this prince then built a Buddhist shrine at Kapisa (in Afghanistan, Central Asia) where he was detained in comfort with all due consideration to his rank. The Chinese prince also donated jewels to this establishment before he returned home.

When Xuanzang (also known as Hiuen Tsang), the famed Chinese pilgrim, visited the Indian subcontinent in the 7th century, he found the walls adorned with paintings of the prince and his companions attired in traditional Chinese garb. It is said that one incidental result of the stay of the hostages in Kanishka's realm was the introduction of the pear and peach, fruits previously unknown in India.

It was a victorious time from Kanishka and the Kushan Empire. Ancient texts, monuments, and inscriptions of this period reveal that the king's reach extended over most of north-western India, and as far south as the Vindhya mountains! It is hardly any wonder then that he soon came to be known as Kanishka the Great.

Kanishka was a supporter of Buddhism and the newer Buddhism of his time was called Mahayana (Great Vehicle). In this version, Buddha was now a god, with numerous Bodhisattvas (Buddha in his previous births) and other beings (such as demigods and *yakshas*) 'mediating' between him and sinful people. The celebrated Gandhara sculptures, of which the best examples date from the rule of Kanishka and his successors, reveal a high level of achievement in the arts at this time. Kanishka's reign also saw the establishment of the fourth Buddhist council, called to compile the scriptures, including the Buddha's

A ROYAL SECRET!

As the Kushans benefited from the Silk Trade route, Kanishka issued gold coins. The Kushans were the first Indian rulers to do so. Another significant development during this time was that horses became a popular choice for the battlefield. Remember the elephant-loving armies of the Nandas and Mauryas?

own teachings. It also saw the preparation of commentaries on all the three *pitakas*, or main divisions, of the Buddhist sacred teachings.

Kanishka's capital was Purushapura (modern-day Peshawar), from where the roads led directly to the plains. It was here in the later part of his reign – after Kanishka had become a Buddhist – that the emperor erected a great tower or stupa holding relics supposedly belonging to the Buddha. Faxian (or Fa-hsien), the Chinese pilgrim who came here 400 years later, described the tower as being made of carved wood, rising up around 13 storeys, almost to 400 ft, and surmounted by an iron pennant. Subsequently, when Song-yun, another Chinese pilgrim, visited it at the beginning of the 6th century, he wrote that this structure had already been destroyed thrice by fire (as it was built of wood) and rebuilt just as many times.

Notably, Kanishka's coins are quite varied. The earliest coins have images of the sun and moon with their Greek names, Helios and Selene. On later issues, the deities depicted are an interesting variety of gods worshipped by the Greeks, Persians and Indians; these also depict the kings themselves, so perhaps the kings now saw themselves as holding divine power.

According to some old texts, there is a strange tale relating to the great emperor's end. It seems Kanishka had a very cunning minister named Mathara. The minister called together all the able generals with their large forces. The king said, 'I have subjugated three regions; only the region of the north (China) has not made its submission.'

Later, the king's people met among themselves and said, 'The king is greedy, cruel and unreasonable; he wants to reign over all four quarters of the world. We must agree among ourselves, and get rid of him.' And as the king was ill, they covered him with a quilt, a man sat on top of him, and the king died on the spot. While it really can't be confirmed if Kanishka was indeed killed in this manner, his reign lasted some 25 or 30 years, and he is regarded as one of India's great monarchs.

WHAT AN IMPACT!

Kanishka was a great conqueror, but he understood that to make one's mark in history, one had to leave behind lasting monuments and objects – and the creations of the Gandhara and Mathura schools of art and sculpture that Kanishka patronized are proof of this.

SAMUDRAGUPTA
Conqueror, King and Poet

After the Mauryas, the second major dynasty to appear in north India was that of the Guptas. It is believed they were initially officials who served under the Satavahanas. As history has shown us, many dynasties began their rise in this way – as subordinates to an old dynasty.

It is believed that the Guptas came from either Magadha or eastern Uttar Pradesh. The first emperor of this dynasty was Chandragupta I (reign: c. 320–330 CE), who took the title of Maharajadhiraja (King of Great Kings). His son Samudragupta succeeded him. From the Allahabad (now Prayagraj) *prashasti* or inscription composed by Samudragupta's court poet Harisena, it appears that Chandragupta I selected the prince from among his other sons.

Samudragupta (reign: c. 330–375 CE) was an all-conquering king. Some of the smaller republics were

A ROYAL SECRET!

In Samudragupta's time, symbols and objects associated with the god Vishnu made their appearance on coins and seals. Historians interpret this to mark the return of Hinduism as the preferred religion.

crushed once and for all. But not all conquered regions were annexed – the distance from Magadha would make defeated territories difficult to rule. So the kings of east India (Samatata in east Bengal and also Kamarupa) and the Himalayan region, as well as smaller states in Punjab, western India and Malwa agreed to pay tribute and to 'obey' Samudragupta's orders.

Having settled the east to his satisfaction, Samudragupta turned his attention elsewhere. From Pataliputra, the Gupta capital, he led his armies down the eastern coast, to conquer the states of southern India – the Dakshinapatha. This move was prompted by the desire to acquire the trading wealth of these regions. And though he was victorious, defeating many a king, he reinstated the vanquished rulers, and made them rule as his subordinates. In a time when communication was primitive and distances long, this made immense sense!

Hearing of Samudragupta's conquests, the rulers in the north and north-west hastened to buy peace with rich gifts. Their acceptance of charters bearing Samudragupta's *garuda* (half man, half eagle; also Lord Vishnu's mount) seal showed their new junior status. It is also clear from Samudragupta's Eran Inscription (in Madhya Pradesh) that he deprived the Vakataka dynasty (who came after the Satavahanas) of some of their territories in central India.

Samudragupta's prestige spread far down south to his Lankan contemporary, King Meghavarna. A Chinese historian relates that Meghavarna sent many gifts to Samudragupta to obtain his permission to erect a monastery at Bodh Gaya for the use of pilgrims.

Despite his image as a great conqueror, there are several references to Samudragupta's love of poetry and music as well. In fact, his coins show him playing the veena. Harisena, the writer of the Allahabad (Prayagraj) *prashasti*, insisted in very flowery terms that the Gupta king was a versatile genius, who pursued the arts alongside all the battles he fought. Samudragupta, indeed, was given the title of 'Kaviraja' (king of poets) for his poetical compositions, none of which have, unfortunately, survived.

WHAT AN IMPACT!

Samudragupta made several conquests, but he knew the effect a symbol had as well. The horse that symbolized a king's power rode through other dominions as part of the Ashvamedha Yagna. Sometimes a symbolic gesture was enough, and many kings in the north and south accepted the greater power of Magadha.

CHANDRAGUPTA II
King of Legends

After Samudragupta, his son Chandragupta II (also Chandragupta Vikramaditya (reign: 375/380–415 CE) ascended the throne. He would go on to become the greatest Gupta ruler! There are several accounts about how Chandragupta II fought off the Saka (the Western Kshatrapa branch) ruler of Gujarat and the Kathiawar peninsula. He dealt them a crushing defeat, killing the enemy king with elaborate deception. The story of this appears in the now lost play *Devichandraguptam*, written by Vishakhadatta.

In this play, Chandragupta II, who is said to be Samudragupta's second son, ascends the throne after the death or murder of his older brother Ramagupta. The story goes that during a battle, Ramagupta was captured by Rudrasimha, the Saka king. The condition for his release was that Dhruvadevi, Ramagupta's wife and the

Gupta queen, surrender herself to the Saka king.

Coin featuring Chandragupta II

Angered by such humiliating terms, Prince Chandragupta disguised himself as Queen Dhruvadevi and entered the Saka king's tent. Once inside, he killed Rudrasimha. Much later, Ramagupta dies, too. According to the story, following the episode of the Sakas, there was a falling out between the brothers. Chandragupta perhaps plotted to kill his brother, as the *Devichandraguptam* mentions. Some historians suggest that Ramagupta may have been a governor or a prince of the dynasty, and not Chandragupta's brother.

In any case, Chandragupta did defeat the Saka king and sealed his conquest with the marriage of his daughter Prabhavati and the powerful Vakataka king, Rudrasena II, who held north-west Deccan. The Vakatakas could be a bulwark to stave off future attacks. The Sakas, however, were shattered and posed no further threat. Prabhavati's marriage to Rudrasena II was vital in another way as well, since Chandragupta's interest also lay in the wealth the area continued to derive from trade with western and south-eastern Asia. The success of his policies was celebrated in a series of silver coins.

Chandragupta II's conquests and daring attack on the Saka satrap turned him into a figure of courage and greatness. He is, at times, identified with the legendary king Vikramaditya of Ujjain, famous in the 'Vikram–

Vetaal' stories. There are several interesting similarities between them. For instance, while the original capital of the Guptas was Pataliputra, Chandragupta made Ujjain his second capital after his western conquests, as it was closer to the north-west border of his empire. The legendary Vikramaditya is also said to have fought the Sakas. And, as per some coins, it is believed that Chandragupta II did indeed take on the title of 'Vikramaditya' (Sun of Valour).

In all the variations of the 'Vikram–Vetaal' story, Vikramaditya always manages to avoid the fate of his many predecessors (because of his wisdom, he is not killed on the day of his coronation, like them) and in time proves to be a great ruler. But then here's the catch: as many as 14 kings in ancient India took on the name Vikramaditya. So no one really knows who the real Vikramaditya was.

Besides being known extensively for his valour, Chandragupta II and his reign are also associated with great cultural and intellectual achievements. These have been described by Faxian (or Fa-hsien), a Chinese Buddhist monk, who travelled in India during 405–411 CE and left a detailed account of his impressions. In Pataliputra, the pilgrim refers to the royal palace of Ashoka (that still stood, 400 years later) and halls, located in the midst of the city, that were built 'in a way no human hands of this world could accomplish'.

About the people of Pataliputra, Faxian says, 'The inhabitants are rich and prosperous, and vie with one another in the practice of benevolence and righteousness.

The Vaishya (trading) families establish houses for dispensing charity and medicines. All the poor and destitute in the country, orphans, widowers and childless men, maimed people and cripples, and all who are diseased, go to those houses, and are provided with every kind of help.'

The Gupta Empire, although less extensive than the Mauryan one, stretched over the northern half and central parts of India. According to Faxian, Gupta rule was mild, benevolent and efficient, the people enjoyed much freedom, and travellers were welcome and safe. No wonder this era was considered to be a Golden Age!

The actual administration, although not as centralized as during the Mauryan period, shared many similarities with it. The feudatory allies had power over the areas they were in charge of. But as in Mauryan times, the head of the state remained the king or raja, assisted by ministers whose office was often hereditary. The Gupta kingdom was divided into provinces (*deshas* or *bhuktis*), and these in turn into smaller units (*pradeshas* or *vishayas*).

The Guptas seemed to like long, impressive titles and designations. Here are some that would never fit into any modern-day business card: the *mahapratikara* (Great Chamberlain), the *mahadandanayaka* (Great General), the *vinayasthitisthapaka* (Minister of Law and Order), and the *bhatasvapati* (Head of the Army and Cavalry). There were even longer ones such as *yuvarajapadtya kumaramatyadhikarana* (Office of the Minister of His Highness the Crown Prince), *ranabhandagaradhikarana*

(Office of the Chief Treasurer of the War Department) and *baladhikarana* (Office of the Chief of Military Forces)!

The Gupta Age saw an interesting variation of religions across its empire at this time. Jainism already had a foothold in present-day Karnataka, Rajasthan and Gujarat. Buddhism flourished in eastern India, with major universities at Nalanda and Vikramashila that attracted large numbers of students. Orthodox Brahmanism (tenets and beliefs coded by the Hindu priestly class) received encouragement, especially from royal families. Learned Brahmins were given endowments of land. This new Brahmanism was focused on the temple. The earliest example of a Hindu temple, in Sanchi, belongs to the Gupta period. This contained a porch and an inner shrine room, called a *garbhagriha*, with an image of the deity. Temples soon came to be gifted with wealth and land, and larger complexes provided education as well. The use of Sanskrit also became popular.

As temples and monasteries thrived, so did the arts, such as mural painting and sculpture, as is evident in the paintings of the Ajanta Caves (in present-day Aurangabad, Maharashtra). Some of the more magnificent caves at Ajanta – nearly 30 rock-cut Buddhist cave monuments with brilliant fresco paintings – were, however, excavated during Vakataka rule. After the Vakatakas, the Chalukyas, who came to power next, continued their patronage. The early paintings are mostly of a crowded world of vegetation and plants, gods and mythical beings, such as *apsaras* and

A ROYAL SECRET!

Chandragupta II's daughter, Prabhavati, married the Vakataka king, Rudrasena II. When he died young, she ruled as regent as her sons were very young. It is one of the earliest recorded instances of a woman wielding royal power.

yakshas, the beauties and bounties of nature, festivals and celebrations. Scenes from Buddhism also appear, especially those from the *Jataka* tales.

The presence of several renowned scholars in this period once led to the speculation that they constituted Chandragupta II's *navaratnas* or nine gems – each endowed with great talent and unique in his chosen field. But while these nine men did live in the Gupta Age (a period of some 300 years), they didn't exist at the same time.

One of these prominent personalities was Kalidasa, whose plays and poems – *Abhijnanashakuntalam*, *Malavikagnimitra*, *Vikramorvashiyam*, *Raghuvamsha* and *Meghaduta* – touched the highest levels of classical literature in Sanskrit. Tradition has it he lived in the court of Chandragupta Vikramaditya.

In mathematics, the Arabs borrowed Indian numerals and introduced them to Europe. Many inscriptions confirm the Indian knowledge of 'zero' and the decimal system.

There was also progress in astronomy. Aryabhata I, writing in 499 CE (in the period of the later Guptas), calculated the correct value of π (pi) and the solar year as 365.3586... days.

Achievements in metal craft were evident in the shape of the Sultanganj Buddha and the very famous Iron Pillar now at Mehrauli in Delhi. The pillar's contours are especially impressive considering it is made entirely of iron and has never rusted.

During the rule of Chandragupta's son and successor, Kumara Gupta (reign: 415–455 CE), there was a new wave of invasions from the north-west. The Huna invasion (from Central Asia originally) challenged the stability of the Gupta kingdom. Their ultimate decline, however, may more realistically have been the result of internal factors, such as feudatories declaring their independence. Nevertheless, the end of the Gupta Age marked the end of one of the brightest periods of ancient Indian history.

WHAT AN IMPACT!

It was under Chandragupta II that ancient India saw its last large empire that extended to both the western and eastern coasts. It would be several hundred years before kings would rule over such an extensive empire, under the Delhi Sultanate.

HARSHAVARDHANA
The Monk Emperor

Among the dynasties that followed the Guptas were the Pushyabhutis (in Thaneswar – present-day Thanesar, Haryana) and the Maukharis (in Kannauj, now in Uttar Pradesh). Harshavardhana (reign: 606–647 CE) came to the throne in Thanesar in very tragic circumstances. He would rule for the next 41 years, and be remembered as a legendary king who ruled both Thanesar and Kannauj.

Most of what we learn about Harsha comes from a book written by the Chinese pilgrim Xuanzang, who visited almost every part of India between 630 and 645 CE. Another work that tells us about the king is a biography, almost a historical romance, called *Harshacharita* (Deeds of Harsha), composed by Bana, who served in Harsha's court – it's also the first historical biography written in Sanskrit and contains, for all its flattery, much information on Harsha's early life.

Harsha's father, Prabhakaravardhana, waged many successful wars against the Hunas. In 604 CE, the king's older son Rajyavardhana led a large army in a campaign against the Hunas. Harsha, then just 15 years old and four years younger to the crown prince, followed his brother with a cavalry force. While in the forests of the Himalayan foothills for some hunting, Harsha received news that his father had fallen dangerously ill. He returned to the capital in haste, but his father died soon after. Barely had Rajyavardhana returned and been duly crowned when a messenger brought distressing news – Grahavarman, king of Kannauj and husband to Rajyasri, sister to the Thanesar princes, had been killed by the king of Malwa. And the princess had been kidnapped.

The young king set off at once with a big army. The Malwa king was defeated with little effort. Treachery, however, was afoot. Shashanka, king of Gaud (Bengal) and an ally of the Malwa king, invited Rajyavardhana to a peace conference and then had him murdered. However, Rajyasri, fortunately, managed to escape to the Vindhya forests.

Learning of his brother's death, Harsha assumed the Thanesar throne reluctantly, and modestly designated himself as Prince Shiladitya; it wasn't until 612 CE that his formal coronation took place. And although he acquired Kannauj (which later became his capital) as a result of his brother-in-law's death, his immediate concern was to avenge his brother's murder and find his sister.

Harsha eventually rescued his sister with the help of local tribes in the Vindhya forests. He also declared war against Shashanka, but parts of his kingdom probably came Harsha's way only after Shashanka's death in 636 CE.

A painting of Harshavardhana

During his rule, Harsha acquired Magadha, Vanga, and Kongoda (now in Odisha). The third was his last recorded campaign, waged in 643 CE. He devoted the last four years of his life to charitable works and to spreading the message of Buddhism, finding the ideal teacher in Xuanzang.

Bana wrote that Harsha devoted his ability and energy to his conquests, with the hope of bringing all provinces 'under one umbrella'. The king is said to have possessed a force of 5,000 elephants, 20,000 cavalry and 50,000 foot soldiers. But perhaps Harsha's heart didn't lie in waging battles.

In 620 CE, the powerful Chalukya ruler of the Deccan, Pulakesin II, defeated him in battle on the banks of the river Narmada. After Harsha's defeat, this river became the new border between the two kingdoms.

Harsha, however, had very good ties with most other kings. His alliance with Bhaskaravarman of Kamarupa (Assam) proved helpful as Harsha engaged in war with Gaud. In the latter years of his reign, Harsha controlled the area around the Ganga river basin (including Nepal). Besides the king of Kamarupa in the east, the king of Valabhi (in modern-day Gujarat) in the west was Harsha's ally as well. And the Tang Emperor of China even sent a series of embassies to Harsha's court to foster closer ties.

Harsha personally supervised the more important things relating to his empire. Except during the rains, when travelling with a huge camp was impossible, he was always on the move, looking into important matters across his realm. Officers maintained records of public events for it was their duty to register 'good and evil events, with calamities and fortunate occurrences'.

When he travelled, Harsha lived in a makeshift 'travelling palace' made of branches and reeds, placed at every stop, and then burned upon his departure. The principal source of revenue came from the rent of the crown lands (owned by the state/king), which amounted to one-sixth of the produce. A quarter of all income was used for government expenses, another quarter for paying officials, yet another for intellectual attainments and charitable works, and the rest for rewards. Some officials were paid by land grants.

Violent crime was rare, but the roads and river routes were evidently not safe, as Xuanzang was robbed more than once. Scholars, who were mainly the Brahmins and Buddhist monks, were honoured and rewarded by the government. In the latter part of Harsha's reign, facilities such as inns, rest houses (dharamshalas), and hospitals were built throughout the empire (towns and rural areas) for the

A ROYAL SECRET!

Harsha was not only a patron of literary talent, but was himself an accomplished calligrapher and an author of some repute. Besides a work of grammar, Harsha apparently wrote three Sanskrit plays. One of his plays, *Nagananda* (Joy of the Serpents) is based on a Buddhist legend and ranks among the best works of Indian drama. His other plays include *Ratnavali* (Necklace) and *Priyadarshika* (Gracious Lady).

benefit of travellers, the poor and the sick. Physicians were stationed at the rest houses to treat the ailing.

Toward the end of his reign, Harsha found himself deeply drawn to Buddhism and ordered the construction of numerous monasteries as well as stupas along the river Ganga. Since these latter structures were made of timber and bamboo, they perished with time.

As king, Harsha was very fond of listening to debates between scholars of different religious sects and spiritual teachers. Harsha, as Xuanzang writes, resolved to hold a special assembly at Kannauj to publicize the Buddha's teachings and to honour Xuanzang. Kings and commoners alike were part of this assembly.

At the end of the proceedings at Kannauj, Harsha invited his Chinese guest to accompany him to Prayag

(Allahabad), the confluence of the rivers Ganga and Yamuna, to witness another elaborate function. Harsha explained that it had been his practice for 30 years past to hold an assembly where he distributed his treasures to the poor and needy, as well as to religious men of all denominations. According to Xuanzang, the generous king gave away all his jewels and clothes, and then begged his sister for an ordinary second-hand garment for himself!

Emperor Harsha died in 647 CE, and after his death, the kingdom of Kannauj entered a period of decline. It was not until the early 8th century that Yashovarman emerged as the new ruler of Kannauj. Although little is known about him, this king is celebrated as a powerful ruler in *Gaudavadha* (The Slaying of the King of Gauda), a Prakrit-language poem by Vakpati, in which Gauda denotes the province of Bengal.

WHAT AN IMPACT!

The battle between Pulakesin II and Harshavardhana established the river Narmada as the border between north and south India. Later dynasties on either side of the river would cross it to lay claim to be a great conqueror. This happened when three dynasties – the Pratiharas, the Rashtrakutas and the Palas – battled one another to emerge as the strongest power. Kannauj became the city of dreams, which dynasties fought to conquer.

PULAKESIN II
The Warrior Who Loved a Contest

Of all the Chalukya rulers, Pulakesin II (reign: 610–642 CE), famous for his victory over Harshavardhana, remains the best-known. The dynasty was founded by his grandfather, a chieftain called Pulakesin I, who, around 550 CE, declared himself the ruler of the area around Vatapi (modern-day Badami) in Bijapur in north Karnataka. His descendants extended the kingdom by annexing coastal areas to the west, thus acquiring important trading ports.

The Chalukya kingdom, south of the river Narmada, occupied an important place in the Deccan. As the plateau's climate is dry in the interior, fertile areas – Vengi, the area drained by the rivers Krishna and Godavari, and the basin of the rivers Krishna–Tungabhadra, known as the Raichur Doab – were often fought over. For 300 years from the mid-6th century onward, the Chalukyas and the Pallavas of Kanchipuram in the south were often at war with each other to control the Deccan and especially the Vengi region.

The prince known as Ereya had to fight a civil war with his uncle, who also claimed every right to be king. Once victorious as king, Ereya called himself Pulakesin II, making a reference to his illustrious grandfather. In the first two decades of his rule, Pulakesin II kept himself busy with his aggressive wars in every direction: on the west and north, the kings of Lata (southern Gujarat), the Gurjara kings (northern Gujarat and Rajputana), Malwa, and small dynasties of the Konkan were defeated, as were the Kadambas and Gangas to the south. After this, Pulakesin turned his attention to the eastern Deccan and conquered trade-rich kingdoms such as Kalinga on the east coast, from where trading ships plied across to Southeast Asia.

He seemed to love a good long fight. At that time, wars were essential to bring more revenue-rich regions under one's control. First, he drove the Pallavas out of the fertile regions of Vengi in the south-east, and appointed his younger brother Kubja Vishnuvardhana viceroy in this region in 609 CE. This marked the beginning of a bitter enmity between the Chalukyas and the Pallavas. These wars between these kings saw a ransacking of each other's possessions, and also the 'stealing away' of artisans and craftsmen to work on their own palaces, temples and capital cities.

In 620 CE came the momentous battle between Harshavardhana and Pulakesin II. Later Chalukya inscriptions refer to this victory over Harsha with great pride. An inscription in old Kannada at Aihole (in Karnataka) records the achievements of Pulakesin II and is even today regarded by historians as a fine literary document.

On returning to Vatapi (Badami) after his war with Harsha, Pulakesin II, still not satisfied, conducted another successful campaign against Mahendravarman, the Pallava king, and won some of the northern Pallava provinces.

At its peak, under Pulakesin II, the Chalukyas ruled quite a big empire. Control over a region stretching across the east and west coasts increased the Chalukyas' firm hold on the Deccan and trading ports.

Pulakesin II's fame even reached Khusru II, king of Persia, who, in the years 625–26 CE, received an embassy, laden with gifts and the offer of friendship, from Pulakesin. In return, Khusru sent an embassy from Persia on his and queen Shirin's behalf, which was received with due honour at the Chalukyan court. A large fresco painting in Cave No. 1 at Ajanta (Aurangabad, Maharashtra) marks the occasion of the arrival of the envoys from Persia and the presentation of their credentials to Pulakesin II.

The wonderful caves in the Ajanta valley were greatly admired by Xuanzang, who visited the court of Pulakesin II, perhaps around 640 CE. The pilgrim was impressed by Pulakesin's military power, and how he was obeyed by his numerous subjects with 'perfect submission'. Xuanzang also wrote that Pulakesin was seen as a good king and his beneficial activities helped a lot of his subjects. The soil was regularly cultivated and was very productive. The people

A ROYAL SECRET!

The battle between Harsha and Pulakesin was fought for reasons that seem familiar even today. Smaller kings/ dependencies posed a threat, or sought the protection of the more powerful ruler, who then had to teach the other power a lesson! One view for the Harsha–Pulakesin battle was the fact that Harsha's growing power may have driven the Latas, the Malavas, and the Gurjaras – in central India – to accept Pulakesin's suzerainty.

were simple and honest. They were fond of learning and very eager to help if asked.

In 642 CE, the long-continued war between the Chalukyas and the Pallavas took another turn. This time it was the Pallava king Narasimhavarman I, Mahendravarman's son, who plundered the Chalukya capital, and Pulakesin II was killed in the battle. The tables had turned. For the next 13 years, the Pallavas had the upper hand in the conflict.

Pulakesin's successors, however, did get the better of the Pallavas after a while. Thirteen years after Pulakesin's death, in 655 CE, Vikramaditya I, Pulakesin's son, inflicted a severe defeat on the Pallavas by raiding Kanchipuram (also known as Kanchi), their strong and fortified capital. But the battles only continued over the next few decades, with victory sometimes favouring one side, and then the other.

A century after Pulakesin II, around 740 CE, another Chalukyan ruler, Vikramaditya II, raced his armies across the Deccan and took over the Pallava capital Kanchipuram. The winning king had an inscription engraved in Kannada on the victory pillar at the Kailasanathar Temple at Kanchipuram to taunt his enemy and mark this conquest. Vikramaditya II was a benevolent ruler. The king's wives also donated to the construction of impressive temples at Pattadakkal, built during the time of Vikramaditya II.

But the 100 years of the Chalukya–Pallava conflict, like the Satavahana–Saka conflict some centuries ago, weakened both sides. No dynasty was ever the ultimate winner. Not long after Vikramaditya II's reign, in 753 CE, Dantidurga of the Rashtrakuta dynasty, a feudatory of the Chalukyas, overthrew the Chalukya king. The Eastern Chalukyas – a branch of the main dynasty – survived longer and were in frequent battle with the Rashtrakutas.

WHAT AN IMPACT!

As many as three Chalukya dynasties ruled southern and south-eastern India, and Pulakesin II was the greatest of their rulers. He waged battles to the south and east, making the small kingdom he had inherited into an empire. Under the Chalukyas, Kannada appears alongside Sanskrit on inscriptions and coins – an indication that the Kannada language flourished during the rule of the Chalukyas.

NARASIMHAVARMAN PALLAVA
The Avenger

Narasimhavarman I (reign: 630–668 CE), also known as Mahamall or Mamalla (the Great Wrestler), was the Pallava ruler in the south, based in Kanchipuram, who continued his dynasty's battle with the Chalukyas. He was known for his strength, especially as a wrestler. Narasimhavarman I was determined to reconquer the territory that Pulakesin II had wrested from his father, Mahendravarman. In a revenge attack in 642 CE, Narasimhavarman swept into the Chalukya capital, Vatapi, with his armies and not just defeated but also killed Pulakesin II. His occupation of the city led to his claiming the title of 'Vatapikonda' (Conqueror of Vatapi).

Like many dynasties, Pallava kings gave themselves an impressive ancestry, dating to King Ashokavarman, who could be the Mauryan king, Ashoka. Historians, however, believe that the Pallavas were first based as small-time rulers around the Kaveri delta (Tondaimandalam), centred at Kanchipuram (ancient Kanchi). Sanskrit and Tamil inscriptions of the later, more powerful, Pallavas show that they rose to power in the 6th century CE. In addition to their bitter rivalry with the Chalukyas, the Pallavas were known for their art and architecture, especially their temples.

Mahendravarman (reign: 600–630 CE), who lost in battle to Pulakesin II, was responsible for the first small rock-cut temples, seen mainly at Mamallapuram, Tamil Nadu. Later, Narasimhavarman I continued his father's work of conquest and art. The monolithic (carved out of a single piece of stone) temples, made of granite, carry the rounded roofs and archways seen in the early Buddhist cave shrines of the Deccan, but the Pallava temples added newer architectural styles. For it was during the reign of Narasimhavarman I's son, Rajasimha (also called Narasimhavarman II) that the beautiful, freestanding (not carved out from hills or mountains) Shore Temple at Mamallapuram was built, as also the Kailasanathar Temple at Kanchipuram.

In Pallava times, villages called the *devadana* or *devadeya* provided revenue to maintain temple life. Their produce or cash from it went towards maintaining the temple and everyone associated with it. Temples also benefited from donations from generous devotees. The bigger temple complexes maintained trained dancers, singers and musicians; the dancers served the deity as *devadasis*.

As per the inscriptions of several Pallava kings and what is gleaned from some land grants, another special category

A ROYAL SECRET!

Xuanzang, the Chinese pilgrim, visited Kanchipuram during the reign of Narasimhavarman I. He writes of there being more than 100 Buddhist monasteries housing more than10,000 monks! There were several Sanskrit colleges as well. The *matha* (a Hindu monastery) was now an important institution, with an educational centre and a rest house too.

of land was the *eripatti* or tank land. The kings understood the vital need for irrigation and revenue from this land went to maintain the village tank.

The Pallavas were powerful not just on land but at sea too. Narasimhavarman I sent two naval expeditions to Ceylon (Sri Lanka) to assist King Manavamma to regain his recently lost throne. The Pallava dockyards at Nagapattinam were used to build ships. The discovery of a possible wharf at Mamallapuram also indicates seafaring activities. The navy assisted in trade with Southeast Asia, which had kingdoms like Kambuja and Funan (Cambodia); Champa (Vietnam); and Srivijaya (the southern Malay peninsula, Java and Sumatra).

During the reign of these powerful Pallava kings (Mahendravarman, Narasimhavarman I and his son Rajasimha), the hymns and poems of Vaishnava (devotees of Vishnu) saints known as the Alvars, and those by the devotees of Shiva (Shaivas) known as Nayanars, became very popular among the people. Appar was the most popular among Shaiva poets, and he converted Mahendravarman from Jainism to Shaivism. The better-known Vaishnava Alvars were Nammalvar, Tirumankai Alvar and the revered woman poet, Andal. Her verses spoke of her love and devotion for Lord Vishnu.

When Rajasimha died in 731 CE, leaving no direct heir, the council of ministers consulted priests to appoint a member of a related branch of the family – King Nandivarman II. The story goes that they travelled to Cambodia in Southeast Asia to request him, then a mere boy of fourteen, to become king. But, in the meantime, the Chalukyas avenged an earlier defeat by allying with the Gangas of south Karnataka. The southern neighbours of the Pallavas, the Pandyas of Madurai, also joined the conflict. In the end, this spelled the end of the Pallavas.

WHAT AN IMPACT!

The Pallavas set the standard for several dynasties that followed. Their interest in the arts, their patronage of temples and support for a navy would be apt examples for the powerful Chola rulers some 400 years later.

AMOGHAVARSHA
The Long-Reigning King

Around 750 CE, the Rashtrakutas, a smaller dynasty in the west, overthrew the last Chalukya king. Among their best-known kings was Amoghavarsha I (reign: 814–878 CE). He was also ancient India's longest ruling king, 'occupying' the throne or being in office (as it would be called today) for around 62 or 64 years – this suggests he came to rule when he was just 14 years old!

Amoghavarsha's predecessors, Dhruva I and Govinda III, waged extensive and expensive wars in the north. They were determined to conquer and hold on to Kannauj, a city that had acquired symbolic value. It had been Harsha's capital, of course, but it was also ideally located on trade routes. Many kings believed that whoever held Kannauj was the master of the universe!

Yet for all the campaigns of Dhruva I and Govinda III in the north, fighting against the Pratiharas, who ruled in central and north-west India, and the Palas of Bengal – dynasties that, along with the Rashtrakutas, desperately sought Kannauj – no one could ever hold Kannauj for long.

Dhruva I, for instance, crossed the river Narmada, marched across central India and conquered Kannauj from the Pratiharas. He then moved south to defeat the Pala king of Bengal. This entire expedition took him four years and a bit longer. But by the time he returned to his kingdom, based around Nashik in present-day Maharashtra and Manyakheta in present-day Karnataka, the Pratiharas had already retaken Kannauj!

Govinda III, his son, followed in his father's footsteps. One of his inscriptions, following his victory over the Pratiharas, proudly stated that his horses 'drank from the icy waters of the Himalayan streams and his war elephants tasted the sacred waters of the Ganga'. Of course, the son made the same mistakes as his father and could not hold on to his extensive conquests for long.

As Govinda III's successor, Amoghavarsha chose a more sensible course of action. For him, the Eastern Chalukyas, a branch of the Chalukyas who ruled over the basin of the rivers Krishna and Godavari, i.e., to the east of the Rashtrakuta kingdom, posed the greater threat. But having spent a large part of his early reign (until 821 CE) in constant wars with the Eastern Chalukyas and other feudatories, Amoghavarsha realized that war was simply not an option. It was a drain of resources and did not help make the dynasty secure.

He was careful, but his policies changed only after he had ensured that his rivals, closer to home, no longer posed a danger. Amoghavarsha I imprisoned the ruler of south Karnataka (from the Western Ganga dynasty), who had been an ally at one time, and some nobles in his own court, who were all implicated in planning a coup against him.

When Vijayaditya II of the Eastern Chalukya family overthrew an ally of the Rashtrakutas, Amoghavarsha I had the excuse he wanted for war. He marched against Vijayaditya II and acquired some Eastern Chalukya strongholds. He then made Manyakheta, already an important city in the east, his capital to guard against future attacks by the Eastern Chalukyas.

Following this victory, Amoghavarsha once again changed his tactics. He now offered peace by way of a marriage settlement between Vijayaditya II's son, Vishnuvardhana V, and Shilamahadevi, a princess from the family of another Rashtrakuta ally.

He used the same tactic to now reconcile the Western Gangas in Karnataka, who had once been his allies. As Amoghavarsha well knew, the closest allies could be the most dangerous enemies. He worked out a marriage between his daughter Chandrabalabbe and the Western Ganga king, Buthuga, and between another daughter, Revakanimmadi, and Prince Ereganga.

In similar fashion, Amoghavarsha I maintained friendly interactions with the Pallavas. His strategy was to always conciliate the enemy after a defeat. His peace terms were

A ROYAL SECRET!

The Arab traveller Sulaiman, who visited Amoghavarsha I's kingdom, described the king as one of the four great kings of the world. It may very well be true since the Rashtrakutas held power for 200 years, and one-third of this period is credited to the wise reign of Amoghavarsha I. It took the powers of three kingdoms – the Chalukyas, the Shilaharas of western Deccan, and then the Cholas – working separately to bring about the end of his successors.

generous. In this way, Amoghavarsha hoped never to create long-lasting hostilities.

After pushing back Arab (and Sidi) raids along the west coast, the Rashtrakutas tried to improve trade relations with them. It worked to their mutual advantage. Shipments of teak and cotton textiles went west, while horses came to India to be sold at great profit to kingdoms further inland. The Rashtrakutas were among the first to employ Arabs at senior administrative levels in the coastal areas.

The long reign of Amoghavarsha proved enriching for the arts, literature and religion of the period. Besides being a soldier and statesman, Amoghavarsha I was an accomplished scholar in Kannada and Sanskrit. His *Kavirajamarga* is an important landmark in Kannada poetics and his *Prashnottara Ratnamalika* in Sanskrit is believed to be a work of high merit. Many Kannada and Sanskrit scholars thrived in his time, including the great mathematician Mahaviracharya, who wrote *Ganita-sara-samgraha* (Compendium of the Essence of Mathematics). There were many other renowned scholars too, such as Jinasena, Virasena, Shakatayan, and Sri Vijaya, who was a Kannada language theorist.

WHAT AN IMPACT!

Amoghavarsha was a practical king. He understood the futility of war, but knew it was necessary and inevitable. As strategy, he ventured out into ambitious conquests farther away only after enemies nearer home had been quelled. He never overextended his empire. After his victories, he always reached out – offering, for example, a marriage alliance – to avert the chance of a future rebellion. In this way, he had the better of the Eastern Chalukyas, the Western Gangas, Pallavas and Arabs. He ensured the longevity of the Rashtrakuta dynasty.

MIHIRA BHOJA
The Multifaceted King

Mihira Bhoja or Bhoja I was the most famous of all the Pratihara rulers who ruled over central India and parts of Malwa in early medieval India (9th century CE). The powerful Pratiharas were long-time rivals of the Rashtrakutas and Palas.

Jain texts, such as the *Kuvalyamala*, speak highly of Mihira Bhoja (reign: 836–885 CE). The Pratihara court patronized the poet Rajashekhara, who wrote eloquently of their glorious ancestry, emphasizing their descent from the *Suryavamsha* (Sun clan) lineage to which Rama, the epic hero of the Ramayana, belonged. Later historians, however, have linked the Pratiharas with pastoral groups who came from the north-west. Their rivals and enemies over time, the Rashtrakutas, insultingly claimed that they were actually *pratiharas* (doorkeepers). The truth possibly lies somewhere in between. Perhaps the Pratiharas were

A ROYAL SECRET!

There were many kings called Bhoja, and one of them – who could be Mihira Bhoja – found the lost throne of Chandragupta Vikramaditya. Like the Guptas, he too adopted the boar as his symbol.

once officials, who served an older dynasty, and eventually came to power.

After fighting off the Arabs (who made their first incursions in the north-west of India in 8th century CE), Bhoja made conquests eastward. Under him and his successors, the Pratihara kingdom included a large part of Rajasthan and Malwa, and also a part of northern Deccan with territories won from the Rashtrakutas. According to Sulaiman, the Arab chronicler, the Pratiharas maintained a large army and had a fine cavalry, and the areas under Bhoja's rule were prosperous and safe from robbers.

Occupied as he was in his efforts to hold back the Arabs in the north-west and the Palas to the east, Bhoja found it impossible to extend his reach much to the south, that is, parts of the Deccan where the Rashtrakutas held control. When he attempted an invasion of the Pala Empire of Bengal, Devapala defeated him. But after Devapala's death, Bhoja attacked again and, this time, succeeded in defeating Narayanapala, the new Pala king, as well as Krishna II, the Rashtrakuta ruler. Bhoja then went on to rebuild his empire by conquering territories in present-day Rajasthan, Gujarat and Madhya Pradesh. Interestingly, the Chandelas of Bundelkhand, who later formed their own kingdom, were initially his vassals.

Bhoja's state was rich in natural resources, as well as in arts and architecture. Many of the temples built during his reign survive even today. For instance, Teli Mandir near Gwalior, Madhya Pradesh, was built to mark where Lord Vishnu, as per mythology, descended to earth. The temple's design shows a mix of different architectural styles: the roof is conical in the Dravidian style of the south, while the motifs and patterns are typical of the north.

Eventually, the endless rivalry amongst these three empires – the Rashtrakutas, the Palas and the Pratiharas – wore these kingdoms out. A hundred years later, the Pratiharas were no longer a power in northern India. And when, coming from the region of Zabulistan (present-day Afghanistan), Mahmud Ghazni's army attacked Kannauj in 1018 CE, it marked the end of Pratihara rule.

WHAT AN IMPACT!

The first wars with the Arabs were repulsed in Mihira Bhoja's time, and he also fought the Palas in the east. These wars meant that the Pratiharas could never reach beyond, into the south.

GOPALA I
An Elected King

There is a story about the first Pala king, who was elected to serve his people. Taranatha, a 16th-century Tibetan Buddhist monk, wrote of this event that took place a long time ago, in his work on the history of Buddhism in India.

It seems Bengal suffered a lot during the days when it was without a king, around 750 CE, a thousand years before Taranatha wrote his book.

Each time the locals elected a king, the chosen person was killed that same night by a demoness. So when Gopala was elected, the goddess Chandi gave him a club to protect himself. He used it to kill the demoness and survived. This hints that Gopala was perhaps a commoner but went on to acquire a kingdom, an event dated to around 750 CE. The story suggests that Gopala was elected because of his ability to protect his people. It also indicates how the local Chandi cult, which Gopala may have supported, became

A ROYAL SECRET!

The artistic style encouraged by the Palas found favour with later dynasties such as the Senas who ruled in eastern India. The Buddha and other divine beings were cast in bronze or depicted on palm-leaf paintings. The bronze sculptures, made via the ancient 'lost-wax process, were rich in depicting the minutest of details. The molten bronze was poured into a wax base, that was drained and melted after the moulds had hardened. Pala bronze sculptures, and the methods used to make them, became popular in Southeast Asia as well.

so very popular in Bengal. Stories, especially old stories, do need to be read between the lines!

In time, the Pala dynasty came to control a large part of the eastern plain of the river Ganga. The Palas also benefited from trade with Kamarupa (Assam) and across the sea towards Southeast Asia. The Palas and the kingdom of Kamarupa were engaged in trade with China through the passes in the eastern Himalayas. The Palas supported Buddhist monasteries, such as Vikramashila and Odantapuri in Bihar, Somapuri in Paharapura (now in Bangladesh) and the most famous of all, the Nalanda university (in present-day Bihar).

The Palas supported and patronized the Buddhist monasteries of Nalanda and Vikramshila by giving them huge grants of villages. During their time, legends and stories of the snake goddess – Manasa – came to be circulated widely.

Still, no dynasty, however powerful, can hold off against conquerors for long. And so, the advance of Rajendra, the Chola king whose successful northern campaign in the early 11th century (1022–23 CE) towards the river Ganga came as a surprise threat, thwarted the plans and borders of Mahipala, the last important Pala king.

WHAT AN IMPACT!

The Palas, in their prime, ruled over a vast area. And for all their wars to seek control of Kannauj, they also reached out into east, west and Southeast Asia. Inscriptions refer to the Abbasid caliphs, who then ruled west Asia and were in contact with the Palas of Bengal. The trade and cultural links between them brought mutual gains. But the attention of the Pala rulers was divided with wars on every side. It was this that would lead to their downfall – with battles first against the Pratiharas and then the Cholas.

ROYAL GALLERY

The Ghaznavids and the Ghurids

The Ghaznavids, who thrived between the 970s to the 1180s CE, became powerful in Central Asia (the regions of present-day Iran, Afghanistan and Pakistan) under Mahmud (reign: 998 –1030 CE). By his sweeping invasions to the west, south and eastward towards South Asia, Mahmud built up a big empire.

Mahmud had secured Ghazni via a fierce battle with Ismail, whom Mahmud's father, Subuktagin, had appointed successor. The Ghaznavids were '*mamluks*' or slaves who swore loyalty to their commanders and rose to lead armies themselves. Mahmud's life was a life of constant battle. He used the motif of religion to rally soldiers to his cause, and he used the plunder and loot to beautify his city of Ghazni. He 'moved' entire libraries from cities of Persia (now in Iran), such as Rey and Isfahan, to Ghazni. He looted temples, most notably that of Somnath in Gujarat, and captured learned people from all over – especially Arabic and Persian scholars from west and Central Asia – to be part of his court at Ghazni. But his last years saw immense conflict with repeated incursions from groups in Central Asia. He had twin sons, Masud and Muhammad, who fought each other bitterly. The later Ghaznavids engaged themselves in bitter fratricidal battles that led to the dynasty's downfall.

The Ghurids followed the Ghaznavids and there is considerable uncertainty and debate about their exact origin. They were based in Ghor, a region west of Ghazni, in modern Afghanistan. They were first subordinate to the Ghaznavids, but in the mid 12th century – around 1150 CE – a local Ghurid leader was killed by the Ghaznavid ruler, one of Mahmud of Ghazni's successors. In the battles that broke out between these two dynasties as either side wanted to exact revenge, the Ghurids finally emerged superior. In one of these battles, the city of Ghazni, so magnificently built up by Mahmud, was set afire and several of its buildings razed to the ground.

Two Ghurid brothers, Ghiyath al-Din Muhammad, and Muizz al-Din Muhammad, ruled jointly between 1173 CE and 1202 CE. They established their hold over Ghazni, and parts of Persia (Iran). Led by Muhammad, the Ghurid armies under their *mamluk* commanders, moved into north India as far as Bengal. These commanders who led mercenary soldiers – men who offered their services to any commander who promised them riches – were motivated by plunder, which they distributed among themselves.

Kannauj, the city that three dynasties – the Pratiharas, the Rashtrakutas and the Palas – had fought over for nearly 150 years, would decline in importance in this period. During the 11th and 12th centuries, it formed part of the Gahadavala kingdom based in present-day north Uttar Pradesh. In 1192 CE, soon after Delhi fell to the Ghurids, Kannauj to the east was attacked as well. Jayachchandra, the Gahadavala ruler, fled toward Benares but was overtaken by enemy soldiers, and killed.

For all the violence he lived by, Muhammad died a violent death himself. It is believed he was assassinated by an ethnic group called the Khokhars in an area around the river Jhelum in 1206. Following this, the Ghurid empire from Central Asia to north India (almost reaching Bengal) was divided among his *mamluks*. Qutbuddin Aibak, one of Muhammad's trusted aides, would go on to establish the Slave dynasty in north India.

TRIBHUVANA MAHADEVI I
The Dutiful Queen

Tribhuvana Mahadevi I was queen of the Bhaumakara dynasty, which ruled parts of present-day central and eastern Odisha from the early 8th century to the mid-10th century. The Bhaumakaras gave themselves a mythical origin, claiming that the Puranas mentioned them from the ancient times. In the early 8th century, the small Bhaumakara kingdom in Odisha's Toshali region was caught in the conflict between the Rashtrakutas to the west and the Palas to the east. Some promise of peace came with the marriage of the Bhaumakara prince, Shantikara I, to Tribhuvana, who was the daughter of Rajamalla, perhaps a Western Ganga king ruling in Mysuru in Karnataka.

When her husband died young, Tribhuvana ruled between 843 and 845 CE as regent for her young son, Subakara III. Her son died soon too, and her grandson Shantikara II only came of age around 863 BCE. So, perhaps,

A ROYAL SECRET!

Tribhuvana Mahadevi II used imperial titles like *Paramabhattaraka, Maharajadhiraja* and *Paramesvan*, just as male rulers did. From the Dhenkanal inscription, it is known that she granted a village Kontaspara to an astrologer for invoking the rains. Later queens Gauri Mahadevi and Dharma Mahadevi also used the same titles.

Tribhuvana Mahadevi I ruled over her small kingdom for a considerably long period.

Tribhuvana Mahadevi was helped by the fact that her father was a powerful ruler at the time, and their combined armies helped quell rebellions and revolts by chieftains and minor feudal lords. The Dhenkanal inscription found in Odisha's western district of the same name describes her as a dutiful daughter, a faithful wife, and a just and kind queen. The state's treasury was used to build temples and tanks. The kingdom taxed its people lightly, and the queen became a much loved and very popular figure. Arab travellers to eastern India, such as Ibn Khordadbeh and Ahmad Ibn Rustah, who came a few decades after Tribhuvana Mahadevi I's rule, sang her praises.

She was known for the Baitala Deula Temple in the city of Bhubaneswar, now Odisha's capital. It was built in an unusual style, with three conjoined shrines, and combined the best stylistic features of Kalinga (ancient Odisha) and Dravidian temple architecture. The spires were high and decorated with carvings and figurines but were semi-cylindrical with a small pointed dome.

Among the later Bhaumakara queens was Tribhuvana Mahadevi II, who was the daughter of a neighbouring king of the Somavamshi dynasty. She ruled briefly in the 890s, before falling victim to palace intrigues. Yet the fact that she ruled in her own right for a while shows the immense respect women wielded as rulers.

A niece-in-law of Tribhuvana Mahadevi II, called Gauri Mahadevi, came to the throne a few years later. It is believed she was regent to her young daughter, Dandi. But Dandi too was overthrown around 916 or 923 CE by her stepmother, Vakula Mahadevi. Soon after, yet another queen, Dharma Mahadevi, came to power. It is believed that both Vakula and Dharma were princesses of the neighbouring Bhanja kingdom, and soon the Bhaumakara kingdom came under the sway of the Bhanjas.

WHAT AN IMPACT!

Tribhuvana Mahadevi I evidently left a mark because royal women of the Bhaumakara dynasty who came after were all skilled administrators and able rulers. There were as many as six Bhaumakara queens who ruled this region, all in the next 150 years.

RAJARAJA CHOLA

An Empire across the Seas

The Cholas were one of India's longest ruling dynasties. They ruled between 300 BCE and 1300 CE (for almost 1,000 years!), and are first mentioned in literature from the Sangam period (4th century BCE to 3rd century CE). The heart of their power lay in the region around the river Kaveri, which flows through Karnataka and Tamil Nadu.

Thanks to King Rajaraja, the greatest king of the Chola dynasty, and his son Rajendra, they were at the peak of their power for nearly 400 years (during 900–1300 CE). In this period, their empire extended over a massive area – it stretched from the islands of Lakshadweep and Maldives in the south/south-west to the northern extent of the river Tungabhadra in modern Andhra Pradesh, and included south India and parts of Sri Lanka! The Chola navy, developed first by Rajaraja Chola and invested in by his son Rajendra, sailed across the seas to eastern India and

Southeast Asia. Their diplomatic missions reached Burma (Myanmar), Malaysia and as far as China.

Mural showing Rajaraja (right) and his guru

In the 50 years before Rajaraja became king, that is, during 950–1000 CE, the Cholas had as many as five kings – and the dynasty was at its weakest at this time. He too might never have become king if family politics had played out differently.

It so happened that the Chola throne was rotating between two rival wings of the family. This contest began with the death of Parantaka I, who had reigned during 907–953 CE. His son Gundaraditya succeeded him. When the latter died, his own son was too young. And so, Gundaraditya's brother Arinjaya came to the throne. It was almost like a game of musical chairs, or rather thrones!

Arinjaya died a year later. His son Sundara succeeded him and ruled for 12 years. Sundara's elder son, Aditya II, was his heir apparent, but was assassinated in mysterious circumstances. Meanwhile, Gundaraditya's son Uttama had reached maturity and now wanted the throne. His mother was the powerful queen mother, Sembiyan Mahadevi. Her word mattered. So Uttama became king, on the condition, however, that upon his death, the throne would not go to his sons; instead, it would return to Sundara's younger son Rajaraja Chola. And so it came to be that in 985 CE, when Uttama died, Rajaraja became the new Chola king.

Considering the many twists and turns in the Chola dynasty, perhaps they were lucky that other kingdoms in their neighbourhood were going through similar unstable times. They might not have survived, otherwise! Once Rajaraja I (reign: 985–1014 CE) came to power, however, he and his son and successor Rajendra extended and strengthened the Chola kingdom, taking it to unimaginable heights.

The reigns of both father and son saw campaigns in every direction. Since conquest was always linked to revenue from trade, Rajaraja wanted to break the alliance between the Cheras in Kerala, the kingdom of Ceylon (Sri Lanka) and the Pandyas of Madurai (now in Tamil Nadu), for these three dominated trade with west Asia.

Although trade with the eastern Roman Empire had long declined, there was a continued demand for pepper and spices in Europe. Arab traders who sailed the Arabian Sea, the Indian Ocean and the East China Sea dominated this trade route and supplied items from Southeast, east and south Asia to the markets of Byzantium (Turkey and North Africa). The Cholas, keen to end Arab competition, especially in Southeast Asian trade, tried to bring the spice-rich Malabar region under their control. A naval campaign, featuring efficient Chola ships with Rajaraja's tiger-emblazoned flag flying high, led to the conquest of the Maldives in the Arabian Sea.

The Cholas also led a campaign in Ceylon (Sri Lanka) destroying Anuradhapura, the then capital, and moved on

A ROYAL SECRET!

Sembiyan Mahadevi was a title taken by many Chola royal queens and consorts (queen mothers, grandmothers, aunts and so on). They were patrons of art and architecture, and active administrators too.

to Polonnaruwa, an area further south. Soon, the spice trade was completely under Chola control – including transit areas and ports of call for the Arab traders and ships before they sailed to Southeast Asia and China.

A campaign against the Gangas and Chalukyas to the north-west meant that the Chola boundary in the north now reached the river Tungabhadra. On the eastern coast, the Cholas battled with the Chalukyas to take control of the fertile Vengi region. It was a repeat of the old conflict between the Pallavas and the Chalukyas.

Despite all the battles, the Chola period was teeming with cultural accomplishments. It was during the 10th century that Queen Sembiyan Mahadevi, Rajaraja's grandmother, initiated the building of large stone temples. But it was Rajaraja I who built the largest temple of the time – the Bhrihadishvara Temple in Thanjavur (Rajaraja's new capital) – from 1003 CE to 1010 CE.

The god Shiva played a lead role in the religious and cultural sphere of the Cholas and their subjects. In fact, the image of the Nataraja or Dancing Shiva in the temples built at this time became symbolic of the Chola period.

Before Thanjavur, Chidambaram (also in Tamil Nadu) was the capital of the Chola dynasty. The Cholas believed that it was the earth home of Shiva and the place where he performed his *ananda tandava* (dance of bliss and destruction). And so, to honour the holy status of this city, the majestic Nataraja Temple was built in the 10th century.

Throughout their rule, different Chola rulers and their queens built several Shiva temples along the river Kaveri. Besides the grand temple at Thanjavur, there was the Gangaikonda Cholapuram Temple in Rajendra Chola's new capital, and the Airavatesvara Temple in Darasuram near Kumbakonam – and all these are part of the UNESCO World Heritage Site known as 'Great Living Chola Temples'.

WHAT AN IMPACT!

The Chola presence – thanks to their trade and military activities – is recorded in Southeast Asia and even China. Under Rajaraja and his son, Rajendra, the Chola navy became powerful in the Bay of Bengal and the east Indian ocean. Rajaraja involved Arabs and Chinese in Chola ship-building activities. The use of this impressive naval force helped Rajaraja dominate the trade to west Asia and towards the east.

RAJENDRA CHOLA
In His Father's Footsteps

Rajaraja ruled for almost 30 years. His son Rajendra I (reign: 1014–44 CE) ruled jointly with his father for two years, and succeeded him in 1014 CE. Like his father, he was a formidable warrior. He was also a shrewd politician, reaching agreements with local rulers and asserting Chola authority over new territories. Thus, he received tribute without the responsibility of direct rule.

Rajendra concluded the battles begun by his father by conquering the southern provinces of the Chalukyas, the rich doab lying between the rivers Krishna and Tungabhadra (in Karnataka), and the Vengi region. This meant more agricultural resources coming to the Chola state. In the south, a revolt against King Mahinda V of Ceylon (Sri Lanka) gave him the pretext to conquer the southern part of the island (the north was already under Chola control).

During 1021–22 CE, Rajendra launched his famous northern campaign. The Chola army and a navy fleet marched and sailed simultaneously along the east coast toward Bengal and then up the river Ganga – almost the reverse of Samudragupta's campaign to Kanchipuram in the 4th century CE. It is said that holy water from the Ganga was carried back to the Chola capital and poured into a Chola temple tank as a symbol of Chola domination over the north. To mark his conquest of kingdoms along the Ganga, Rajendra also built a new capital called Gangaikonda Cholapuram. Despite his great success, Rajendra did not hold on to the northern regions for long, a situation again paralleling that of Samudragupta's campaign in the south, almost 700 years earlier.

Rajendra's overseas campaign was even more ambitious, involving the use of his powerful navy against the kingdom of Srivijaya (areas of Java and Sumatra in Indonesia). His desire to protect Chola trade interests was the supposed reason for the war. By the 10th century, merchants in China and south India had trading relationships with the Srivijaya kingdom. Ships headed to China passed through the seas held by Srivijaya rulers. These rulers realized it would be profitable for local traders if the China–India trade ended at Srivijaya's ports, and local traders then transported the goods to their eventual destinations. Tamil and other merchants from India (from Kalinga, for instance), who travelled farther and had their own contacts in the Srivijaya kingdom, saw their business thus threatened.

A ROYAL SECRET!

A foremost example of Chola art is the stylized bronze idol of goddess Parvati or Uma. Famous literary figures in the Chola period include the poet Kambar/ Kamban, famed for his *Kamba Ramayanam*, the Tamil version of the epic Ramayana, while the works of poets Jayamkondar and Ottakuttan depict events during the reign of King Kulathunga Chola 1. Women poets and singers of hymns dedicated to the worship of Vishnu or Shiva were also known – Akkamahadevi of the 12th century was one such renowned poetess.

At that time, merchant associations or guilds had a lot of say. Many a time, they influenced royal decisions on trade and conquests. They often financed local projects, for example, the building of a temple, and even extended loans to kings and royalty. Chola rulers too invested well in trade – indeed, the royal family, including the queens, had a share in sea trade. Hence, the ire of the merchant associations and the Chola king's own concerns led to an attack on Srivijaya. The campaign was successful as several strategic ports came under Chola control, and, for a while at least, Chola ships had safe passage through the seas here.

This victory permitted, over the next few decades, an improvement in the commerce of south India and better communications with the Chinese. Elephants, horses, spices, perfumes, precious stones and high-quality textiles were the goods involved in such trade; metalwork, jewellery, pottery and salt (produced in salt pans from seawater) were somewhat less important, and largely along the east coast of India. A later successor to Rajendra Chola, Kulottunga I, sent an embassy of 72 merchants to China in 1077 CE!

In their last years, almost 100 years after Rajendra Chola's rule, the continued raids by the Hoysalas and the Pandyas into their territory weakened the Cholas. And as it happened often in history, the Chola dynasty ultimately came to an end.

WHAT AN IMPACT!

From around the 9th century CE, the ancient Indian epic, Ramayana, became greatly popular in Southeast Asia, in the regions of Java and Cambodia. Ships, especially those from the Chola navy, sailed eastward. Scholars, merchants and travellers helped disseminate the stories of the Ramayana that were soon adapted and incorporated into diverse cultural forms such as dance and plays. The first literary version of the Ramayana written in old Javanese dates to the early 10th century CE. The stories of the Ramayana continue to be popular in Bali, an Indonesian island, via its shadow puppet tradition.

PRITHVIRAJ CHAUHAN
A Legendary Ruler

There are kings who leave behind records. Then there are kings whose lives are a mix of legend and fact. And then there are kings who, in the course of time, become larger-than-life. Prithviraj Chauhan, the ruler of Delhi and Ajmer at one time, was a king who can be listed in the last category.

Sometime around 1150 CE, the Chauhan kings replaced the ruling Tomaras of Delhi. Interestingly, it is Anangapala, the Tomara king, who is credited as having founded one of the many cities that later (all combined together) came to be known as modern-day Delhi. Some historians believe that in 1052 CE, Anangapala had Chandragupta Vikramaditya's famous Iron Pillar shifted to its current location in Mehrauli in Delhi.

The Chauhans were among the four important Rajput clans of this time. The Chauhans, Pratiharas (different

A ROYAL SECRET!

Prithviraj's rivalry with Jaichand, the king of Kannauj, is legendary. As one enduring story goes, Prithviraj was not invited to the *swayamvara* – when princesses chose their husbands from an assembly of princely suitors – of Jaichand's daughter, Samyukta. Instead Prithviraj's statue was placed at the entrance as a doorman. It was an insult, but Samyukta garlanded the statue, and the real Prithviraj sprang from behind it, where he had been hiding all the while, and galloped away with her.

from the ones before), the Chalukyas of Gujarat (again a different dynasty) and the Paramaras, all claimed that their ancestor had emerged from a huge sacrificial fire pit near Mt Abu in Rajasthan. The most famous of the Chauhans was Prithviraj or Rai Pithora (reign: 1166–92 CE), who became famous in song and legend as a chivalrous warrior, lover and tragic hero. Prithviraj's legend rests on his daring kidnapping of Samyukta, the daughter of his rival Jayachchandra (Jaichand), king of Kannauj, in or about 1175 CE – a story immortalized by the epic poem *Prithviraj Raso* by Chand Bardai; it is, however, believed to be composed some 400 years after Prithviraj.

Prithviraj's reputation as a warrior also rests on the story of his defeat of the Chandela king and capture of the city of Mahoba in 1182 CE. But his heroism largely stems from the resistance he offered to Muhammad of Ghor.

Muhammad, the ruler of Ghor in Afghanistan, began his series of invasions in the late 12th century, a hundred years after Mahmud of Ghazni, another ruler from the north-west, had made several plundering raids into Gujarat and north India. In 1191 CE, Prithviraj succeeded in inflicting a severe defeat upon the Ghurid forces at Tarain (between Thanesar and Karnal in today's Haryana). This forced the Ghurid armies to retire beyond the river Indus.

A year later, however, in 1192, Muhammad of Ghor returned to once again face Prithviraj. This time, the Arabs were victorious. It is believed that Prithviraj was taken prisoner and then executed. But the *Raso* narrates that Prithviraj was captured and blinded. Chand Bardai, his court poet, then tricked Muhammad of Ghor to set up an archery performance by the blind king. Taking advantage of this, Prithviraj aimed his arrow at Muhammad of Ghor based on the sound of his voice and felled him instantly. Prithviraj died soon after for this act, but his martyrdom would live on forever.

WHAT AN IMPACT!

Rulers of Mewar and Marwar in the 16th century traced their linkages to the brave king Prithviraj, to stress the longevity and glory of their own dynasty.

ROYAL GALLERY

The Eastern Gangas

The Eastern Ganga (or Chodaganga dynasty) kingdom, centred in Utkala and Kalinga in present-day Odisha, is mainly known for its impressive stone temples, such as the Jagannath Temple in Puri. Anantavarman Chodaganga, who stressed his matrilineal linkages to the Chola dynasty, built this acclaimed and holy structure. His rule extended from north-east (present-day) Andhra Pradesh to a large part of Odisha along the coast.

The Ahoms of Kamarupa

Further east, Kamarupa in present-day Assam was a kingdom in the Brahmaputra River Valley, but close to the mountains. It provided an important link between eastern India, and Tibet and China, and this encouraged trade as well as the movement of pastoral groups and pilgrims across the mountains. Rice cultivation was popular in this land watered by the river Brahmaputra. The Varman dynasty was the first to bring a part of the Brahmaputra

Valley under its control in the 1st millennium CE. Its most renowned king was Bhaskaravarman (reign: 600–650 CE), who was a friend and ally of Harshavardhana; the Chinese pilgrim Xuanzang left behind accounts of him.

In the 13th century, the Ahoms, a people of the Shan ethnic group, who came across the mountain passes from lands south-east of Assam, conquered much of Kamarupa. It was they who gave the place its name, Assam – derived from Ahom. Their other contribution was the maintenance of lengthy genealogical records, the *burunjis*, which help in the reconstruction of their history. The Ahoms were also one of the longest ruling dynasties of India, lasting till the 19th century, when wars with the British for control of the north-east led to their defeat.

The Queens of Kashmir

It was around 8th century CE that Kashmir saw the rise of King Lalitaditya of the Karkota dynasty. The ruler's attempts, however, to establish a foothold in the northern Indian plains were not successful, for in his battles with Yashovarman, the king of Kannauj, no clear winner emerged. So both kings held on to their respective territories, and no one won or lost any territory (though, of course, many lives and much wealth was always lost in such wars and battles).

The 10th century saw two famous queens acting as regents. They rose to power at different times in this century, and, despite the opposition to their rule, came to play a vital role in state affairs. Both queens had to counter a new phenomenon that dominated Kashmir's politics in this time – the rise of troops or warriors who held their own political loyalties and ambitions. There were two rival warrior groups: the Tantrins and the Ekangas – each played the role of king (or queen) makers in Kashmir.

The first of these regents was Queen Sugandha, who allied with the Ekangas and used them against the Tantrins. She meant to play off one group against the other, but she was not successful and was deposed in 914 CE. Her defeat meant almost unlimited power for the Tantrins, and the rulers who followed had no way of opposing them. Finally, the *damaras* (feudal chiefs or powerful landlords) had to be called in to destroy the Tantrins and their power.

The *damaras* had been helped in their rise to power by developments in agriculture, mainly through the irrigation and drainage policies put into effect by Suyya, a high-ranking minister in the court of King Anantivarman in the 9th century CE. Suyya had the rivers Jhelum and Indus cleared of debris by building earthen reservoirs to prevent mud dumped by landslides from flowing into the rivers. His endeavours also ensured that the region was safe from recurring floods and, as a result, made more land available for cultivation. The surplus that was then possible in rice and products like saffron gave the *damaras* a lot of power, and as powerful landlords, they were now determined to have a say in governance. The 12th century writer Kalhana describes them in his *Rajatarangini* (River of Kings), which chronicles the history of Kashmir, saying that they soon employed mercenaries to add to their power and began throwing their weight around.

The *damaras* were so successful that the rulers of Kashmir were now faced with the new problem of restraining their clout – a problem that manifested itself during the reign of the next notable regent of Kashmir, Queen Didda. She ruled as regent not just for her son but for two of her grandsons as well. The *Rajatarangani* records that power went to Didda's head. It was rumoured that she had her youngest grandson, who was then the actual ruler, killed. But she was able to keep the *damaras* at bay with her own supporters and gave Kashmir a period of much-needed stability.

Indeed, it was not unheard of for queens to rule as regents, as Prabhavati Gupta had done in the Vakataka period, or to carry out administrative functions, as in the case of some Chalukya queens of the western Deccan. Sugandha and Didda triumphed during the period of their rule over the factionalism that prevailed among the nobles and officials, and in this time managed to carry out impressive work that helped their subjects.

ILTUTMISH
A Practical Sultan

Around 12th century CE, Muhammad of Ghor (based in Ghazna in present-day north Afghanistan) invaded India in the hope of expanding his realm. The sultan's famous battles were against the Chauhans (Prithviraj) in 1191 and then in 1192; the latter battle led to the Ghurids' (an ethnic group from present-day Central Asia) decisive victory. Muhammad of Ghor then made a few more conquests in the north and north-west before returning to Ghazna with a large treasure. He left Qutbuddin Aibak, his slave (*mamluk*) and trusted lieutenant, in charge of consolidation and further expansion. In 1206, however, Muhammad was unexpectedly assassinated in Lahore, a city that was part of his kingdom. After his death, Qutbuddin Aibak became the sultan of Delhi, and founded the Mamluk or Slave dynasty.

In 1210, only four years after Muhammad of Ghor's death, Qutbuddin Aibak died in a polo accident. Taking

A ROYAL SECRET!

It was Iltutmish who completed the Qutub Minar in present-day Mehrauli, Delhi, begun by his father-in-law and the first ruler of the Slave dynasty, Qutbuddin Aibak. The minar and the Quwwatul Islam mosque in the same complex were built in honour of a Sufi saint, Qutbuddin Bhaktiar Kaki. Later rulers like Firuz Shah Tughlaq and Sher Shah Suri made their own additions to it.

advantage of the situation, his slave and son-in-law, Iltutmish (reign: 1211–36 CE), ascended the throne of the Delhi Sultanate, a region comprising Delhi and the area around it. Almost immediately, Iltutmish was faced with three main concerns: Genghis Khan, the dreaded Mongol leader, threatened the north-west; his fellow nobles of Turki origin (from Turkmenistan) always threatened to break away and form their own independent kingdoms; and neighbouring kingdoms around Delhi posed a severe threat as well.

As far as Genghis Khan was concerned, Iltutmish decided to play a waiting game against the Mongols since their armies, at that time, were simultaneously engaged in threatening other dynasties in west and Central Asia. Iltutmish cunningly ignored the requests for help by these kingdoms that faced the Mongol onslaught. Instead, he turned his attention to the east, where he managed to conquer north Bengal. In the west, however, his campaigns in Rajasthan, and central and western India were not as successful, and he could not hold on to the forts of Ranthambore, Mandsaur and Gwalior. These latter two places symbolized that a ruler dominated the north and could pose a threat to the southern kingdoms.

However, by the time Iltutmish died in 1236, he had placed the Delhi Sultanate, at least in its immediate environs, on a more secure footing. The sultan had also been wise in how his kingdom was run. He knew he ruled over a mixed population, and so Islamic law (*sharia*) could not be imposed on the majority, and he made this clear to the clerics (*ulema*) and the nobles. He also insisted that laws had to be interpreted according to local customs. Iltutmish's independence of thought is reflected in the fact that after his favourite son, Nasiruddin, died in 1229 (he was governor of Bengal at the time), he nominated his daughter, Razia, to succeed him. Iltutmish believed that his sons were not very capable of ruling. Razia, moreover, had been trained to be a strong ruler. She would be the first woman ruler of Delhi.

WHAT AN IMPACT!

Faced with the threat of the Mongols, Iltutmish chose to focus on his kingdom around Delhi and the area around it. From these early beginnings, the Sultanate extended its reach, in due course, over the whole of north India.

RAZIA
'Sultan'

For all of Iltutmish's wishes, soon after his death in April 1236, the powerful coterie of Turkish nobles, dubbed the Chahalgani (The Forty), nominated Razia's brother, Ruknuddin-Firuz, to the throne. Ruknuddin spent his time in drinking and debauchery. It was Shah Turkaan, his mother and Iltutmish's widow, who controlled matters. Barely six months later, in November 1236, Ruknuddin and his mother Shah Turkaan were assassinated.

It was then that Razia (reign: 1236–40 CE), in accordance with her father's wishes and to the great chagrin of most of the nobles, came to the throne. She was experienced in the practicalities of administration, thanks to her father. She had also learnt to effortlessly ride an elephant and a horse. The nobles could not get past the fact that a woman was ruling over them. Moreover, Razia dressed like a man and insisted on being addressed as Sultan. This must have scandalized the nobles no end. She was also resented for her determination to keep control over the realm, and keep the nobles in their place. Thus, they were determined to find a more pliable monarch in place of Razia.

Razia ruled over a kingdom that included Delhi, parts of present-day Haryana, Punjab, northern Uttar Pradesh and the northern parts of Rajasthan. Initially, she was able to effectively manipulate rebel factions against each other. In a matter of months, however, a war broke out when some of her nobles vocally opposed her choices. They resented her growing closeness to one of her advisers, Jamal-ud-din Yaqut, a slave of Abyssinian origin. Yaqut was an expert horseman and Razia first appointed him as the superintendent of the stables, and then promoted him as Amir al-Umara (commander of commanders).

The nobility could not hold back their fury any more when a slave was placed in such a high position and an open rebellion broke out. Some of the provincial governors refused to accept Razia's authority. In 1240, the governor of Lahore rebelled. But Razia did not give up easily. The governor of Lahore had to retreat as far as the river Chenab and was then forced to surrender.

Soon after, another rebellion broke out in Bhatinda in Punjab under another noble, Malik Altuniya. A battle between Razia and Altuniya followed, with the result that Yaqut was killed and Razia taken prisoner. In a settlement with Altuniya, who wanted a share of the power, Razia was forced to marry him. But by this time, in Delhi, the

A ROYAL SECRET!

The myth of Razia has only grown. There have been two films made on her: in 1961 – starring Nirupa Roy as Razia and directed by Devendra Goel – and 1983, when Kamal Amrohi directed the film and Hema Malini played the lead role. A television serial, *Razia Sultan,* made in 2015, became popular not just in India, but also in Indonesia, Mauritius and Germany!

Chahalgani had appointed Razia's brother, Muizuddin Bahram Shah, as a puppet king.

Time was running out for Altuniya and Razia. Unable to find much support for their cause, they were defeated in battle in October 1240. Razia and her husband then fled to the outskirts of Delhi and reached Kaithal (in Haryana) the next day, where their remaining troops abandoned them.

Not one to give up, Razia then attempted to advance with the help of a local tribe known as the Khokars. Historians believe that Razia, and Altuniya, were likely killed by the Khokars or by wandering thieves.

Razia ruled for just three years, from 1236 to 1239. Her successors, placed on the throne by the conspiring nobles, did not last long. Seven years after Razia's death, in 1246, it was Iltutmish's grandson, Nasiruddin (who had the same name as his father, Iltutmish's son), who came to the throne. He was kind and scholarly, and led the simple life of a Sufi saint, copying the Quran to pay for his needs.

In effect, it was left to Nasiruddin's trusted deputy Ghiyasuddin Balban to restore the fortunes of the Sultanate. Balban became sultan after Nasiruddin's death in 1266, and his first move was to thoroughly clip the powers of the Chahalgani. Under Balban, the Delhi Sultanate saw off several Mongol invasions. He also ruthlessly suppressed a revolt in Bengal, chasing the rebel noble Tughril across rivers and regions. Balban also tried to raise the prestige of the institution of the Sultanate by elaborate ceremony and strict insistence on justice, but he failed to develop a loyal support base. And so, when he died in 1287, the Slave dynasty collapsed, making way for the Khiljis.

WHAT AN IMPACT!

When Iltutmish made Razia his successor, it showed that he was independent in his thinking from either the rulers of west Asia and the Caliphate in Arabia. Razia became the first woman ruler in north India (and in the Islamic world).

RUDRAMA DEVI
Warrior Queen of Warangal

In the same century as Razia, another brave queen emerged in the Deccan: Rudrama Devi, who reigned as queen almost 50 years after Razia Sultan.

When the Italian traveller, Marco Polo, reached south India in the late 13th century, he had already heard a lot about Warangal and the fabled wealth of its mines. Marco Polo described Warangal as an inland kingdom. But the king Pratapa Ganapati Rudra Deva of the Kakatiya dynasty had made conquests along the eastern coast, right up to present-day Nellore in north Tamil Nadu and also north towards the frontier with what is now Odisha.

Ganapati Rudra Deva had no male heir, and it was his daughter, Rudrama Devi, who ruled Warangal for almost 28 or, as some records suggest, thirty-eight years. For a long time there was confusion about whether Rudrama

A ROYAL SECRET!

Rudrama's bravery, generosity and charisma were well captured in *Rani Rudrama Devi*, a Telugu 3-D period action film made in 2015 by Gunashekhar. The actor Anushka Shetty played the role of the queen.

was Ganapati's daughter or wife. Historians generally accept that she was his daughter.

Marco Polo described a settlement of merchants from Genoa and Venice on the eastern coast, who traded in diamonds and fine cloth for which Warangal was famous. The rulers of Warangal were also known to be liberal in their religious endowments, donating to temples dedicated to various Hindu gods, and to Buddhist and Jain shrines as well. Ganapati Rudra, who died in 1257, was known to be a great king. Chronicles of the time praised him as an apt successor to the valiant Satavahanas who had ruled over this region a thousand years ago.

Rudrama Devi, like Razia Sultan, was raised like a warrior prince. It appears that she called herself Rudra Deva. Soon after her succession, she was able to successfully quell revolt and mutinies from minor chiefs. She also effectively managed the much weakened Cholas in the south and the Yadavas of Devagiri to the west. Rudrama ensured this by managing the army well. She sought out warriors from various groups and affiliations, and paid them a share of the land tax, so that they would not be lured away by minor rulers and chiefs.

Rudrama was a generous patron of the Thousand Pillared Temple or Rudreshwara Swamy Temple, built on the hills of Hanamkonda in present-day Telangana. The temple had three shrines dedicated to Shiva, Vishnu and Surya. Every pillar in the temple was carved exquisitely and carefully by skilled craftsmen.

She also completed the building of the Warangal Fort, improved the tank irrigation system, and set up dispensaries to assist the ailing. Historians suggest that she used a traditional dance form, the 'Perini Shiva Tandavam', as a training method for soldiers.

There has been a long-running debate over how the courageous Kakatiya sovereign met her end. Recent discoveries of two sculptures apparently representing Rudrama have been made in a village in Warangal district, now in Telangana. Historians believe that the two 'sequential sculptures' suggest that she died while fighting a dissident chieftain called Ambadeva.

WHAT AN IMPACT!

The fort of Warangal was for long one of the most undefeatable forts in Indian history. For the next 500 years, forts construction – such as Tipu Sultan's fort at Srirangapatna – would emulate Warangal.

ALAUDDIN KHILJI
A Powerful King with a Love of Gold

On 13 June 1290, Jalaluddin Firuz Khilji staged a successful coup and brought an end to the Slave dynasty, bringing the Khiljis to power. But he was assassinated just six years later in 1296 by his ambitious nephew and successor, Alauddin Khilji (reign: 1296–1316).

Alauddin Khilji, who had led many campaigns on behalf of his uncle, knew that the established nobility regarded his family as 'inferior'. He turned to 'outsiders' to assist him in his game of power. Some of these outsiders were those nobles from Central Asia who had escaped Mongol attacks and came to seek service in the Delhi Sultanate. There were others from the native elite as well – from landed families in western and northern India. Alauddin knew he needed money – lots of it – and gold too. This would buy him a loyal and submissive nobility, and an efficient army under his absolute control.

While commanding his uncle's armies, Alauddin had solved this problem by looting enemy provinces. For instance, in 1292, he raided the rich region of Bhilsa in central India. Then in 1296, he led an unauthorized raid on the wealthy city of Devagiri (present-day Daulatabad), the capital of the Yadavas in the Deccan. The wealth of Devagiri not only helped him finance his plan to usurp the throne, it got him even more support. The story goes that as Alauddin approached Delhi with his army, gold coins were showered at random on the crowds of onlookers, simply to win them over.

As sultan, Alauddin needed a secure source of income that would help him ensure the loyalty of his soldiers and groups of nobles. A strong army was also essential to fight off the ever-present Mongol threat. The Mongols had already reached the areas beyond Punjab. In 1303, Delhi experienced a two-month long siege.

At the time, the state had four sources of income – land revenue (then one-fifth of the produce); booty from war (of which the sultan usually claimed the largest part); *jizya,* a tax imposed on non-Muslims (so the state treasury benefited if people did not convert); and a contribution from Muslims for charitable works. For a proper assessment of the land revenue Alauddin ordered his officials to make an estimate of agricultural produce by a strict reassessment of the land. This, of course, was in the region around Delhi, Punjab and parts of the Doab (the Ganga–Yamuna plains). He set the land tax at half the produce (in weight or value) of each peasant's holding, regardless of size. This would be supplemented by a house and cattle tax. The nobles (high-ranking commanders and officials) had the right to collect revenue from land, but did not own the land itself. From this revenue, they had to maintain foot soldiers and cavalry. These revenue holders or *iqtadar*s could be transferred. The *khalisah*, or crown lands, whose revenues went directly to the sultan's treasury, was expanded greatly, which helped the sultan pay a much larger number of his soldiers and cavalry troops in cash.

These measures were followed by price regulations in the area around Delhi. Prices of grain and cloth were regulated and fixed. Grain, especially, was maintained at a low price. The state granaries had buffer stock, which, along with price caps, solved the problem of maintaining a large standing army. This also helped keep the citizens, at least of Delhi and its immediate regions, satisfied.

In order to ensure a good and regular supply of horses from Arabia, Alauddin extended a large loan to the merchant group known as the Multanis (from Multan in Sindh), who together with the Khorasanis (from Persia) controlled the long-distance overland trade. Cavalry now made up an important segment of the army, and horses were imported in large numbers from this time onward.

With the objective of expanding his own support base, Alauddin offered positions and service to diverse groups in the country. He reached out to native nobles and Hindus as well. Both Alauddin and his son married into the families of important local rulers.

Alauddin's expansion plans began with the conquest of Gujarat in 1299. He then moved into the area now in present-day Rajasthan and captured the long-impregnable fort of Ranthambore (1301). From there he moved on to Chittor (1303), and Mandu in central India (1305). The story of his conquest of Chittor is mired in a lot of legend and myth.

For Alauddin, the campaigns in Rajasthan were just steps towards the Deccan and the south. The southern states were aflush with wealth, thanks to their trade relations with west and Southeast Asia. Beginning with the Kakatiya kingdom of Warangal, Alauddin's army, led by his trusted slave and lieutenant Malik Kafur, whom Alauddin had recruited in Gujarat, subdued the Yadava kingdom of Devagiri (in the Deccan), the Hoysalas (in Karnataka), and then the Pandyas of Madurai.

In the end, Alauddin's efforts to have a strong, secure and loyal army paid off. With his victories in the south, he secured immense wealth in the form of tribute. He knew annexing these regions and ruling them from faraway Delhi would make the empire unwieldy, hard to manage and vulnerable to rebellion.

The armies of the Delhi Sultanate destroyed the Yadavas dynasty. This time, Malik Kafur, Alauddin's trusted slave commander, arrived in Devagiri at the head of the Khilji army around 1308–09 CE. Ramachandra, still king, once again submitted to the invader, once again paying a lot in tribute. After his death some years later, his son-in-law, Harapala, tried to revolt in 1318, but was defeated, and executed on Alauddin's orders.

In 1303, Alauddin's first attempt to conquer Warangal ended in a disaster. Its sturdy, multi-walled fort made of granite, secured by moats and bastions, was virtually impossible to conquer. But Warangal was eyed by every conqueror worth his salt, as its mines produced precious stones, like diamonds, that were in great demand.

In 1309, Malik Kafur, Alauddin's general, invaded Warangal and was able to defeat King Prataparudra and occupy the famous fort with the help of 1,00,000 soldiers. The vanquished king was forced to pay an indemnity, including much of the fabled Warangal treasury, with its horde of diamonds and precious jewellery. He also had to acquiesce to pay an annual tribute to Alauddin.

Following this, Alauddin was set on attacking the Hoysala kingdom. Founded some 200 years or so before the Khiljis became rulers of north India, the Hoysalas ruled a region now in modern Karnataka. They were known as a dynasty of very brave kings. Ballala II, who had the epithet 'Veer' (brave) before his name, was the Hoysala king who faced off Malik Kafur when he arrived in the vicinity with his huge army. He was also famous for having single-handedly fought off a lion!

The Khilji army ransacked and raided, but had no desire to rule. They realized that the distance from Delhi was

A ROYAL SECRET!

The epic poem *Padmavat*, which tells of Alauddin's battle with Chittor's heroic king Ratan Sen over his queen, Padmini, known for her beauty, was written 240 years or so after Alauddin's time, by the poet Malik Mohammad Jayasi in 1540. The poem is seen by scholars as a metaphorical work on Sufi thought and the first work in Avadhi.

too much for effective governance. The Hoysala capital Halebid (or Dorasamudra) was sacked twice. The Hoysala temples at Halebid, Belur and Somanathapura were the main targets since they were known repositories of wealth.

The Pandyan kingdom lay south and east of the now decimated Hoysalas. The Pandyas were among the oldest southern dynasties. Their kingdom was established in southern Tamil Nadu, based around Madurai. The Pandyan kingdom was small yet prosperous, thanks to its strategic position in the south. Its ports dominated the trade across the Bay of Bengal, and drew in merchants from Arabia in the west and China to the east. Marco Polo, who visited the Pandyan kingdom in 1288 and 1293, left a vivid description of the richness of the land and the large and beautiful pearls found in its seas.

Not surprisingly, the realm's prosperity drew the attention of the Sultanate armies, and soon enough, after his victories over Devagiri and Warangal, Malik Kafur arrived on his treasure hunt on the sultan's behalf. The Khilji general plundered the Pandyan kingdom during 1310–11 CE – an invasion described in some detail by the Sufi poet and mystic Amir Khusro. Malik Kafur outwitted his enemy in the battlefield by clever planning and better-equipped soldiers, but a portion of the Pandyan army barricaded itself inside the temple town of Madurai. For all his efforts and use of battering rams, Malik Kafur was unable to break through the strong defensive walls, and in the end had to lift his siege and return to Delhi.

Despite all the plunder and for all the wealth he accumulated, Alauddin did not leave behind strong successors. Jealous rivals killed Malik Kafur, and the Tughlaqs soon replaced the Khiljis.

WHAT AN IMPACT!

Under Alauddin Khilji, the Sultanate extended its reach deep into south India through the better preparedness of its armies and the promise of gold. His conquests set an example for later rulers of north India, who would seek to reach into eastern and southern India, rather than focus on west Asia.

MUHAMMAD BIN TUGHLAQ
King of Bad Decisions

Muhammad bin Tughlaq came to the throne of Delhi in 1325, barely nine years after Alauddin Khilji's death. In this time, the Tughlaqs had replaced the Khiljis. Ghiyasuddin Tughlaq, one of Alauddin's high officials ruled for only five years (1320–25) and there was a rumour that his death was his son Muhammad bin Tughlaq's doing.

Right from the beginning of his rule, Muhammad bin Tughlaq (reign: 1325–51 CE) made some spectacularly poor decisions. He inherited a kingdom that, centred in Delhi, spread over a large part of north India including areas in Punjab, eastern and south Rajasthan, north Uttar Pradesh and Madhya Pradesh today. Problems began when he wanted to bring the southern powers under the direct control of the Delhi Sultanate, instead of keeping them as tribute-paying states. He soon realized (as many of his predecessors had!) that direct rule over the south was impossible, given the distance from Delhi. It was thus that the sultan decided to make Daulatabad (earlier called Devagiri) in the Deccan his second capital. The move was also to gain access to the western and southern ports, and have a capital that would be secure from future invasions from the north-west.

Muhammad bin Tughlaq orders brass coins to pass for silver

Much about Muhammad bin Tughlaq's reign is known from Ibn Batutah's account. When Batutah was 21 years old, in 1325, he left his home in Tangier in Morocco, Africa, to travel the world. He wrote a detailed account of his travels in west Asia, the Indian subcontinent, Ceylon (Sri Lanka) and the Maldives in the *Rehla of Ibn Batutah* (*rehla* means journey). Ibn Batutah stayed in India for about 14 years of which about eight were spent in Delhi (1334–42) during the rule of Muhammad bin Tughlaq. The sultan, impressed with his learning, appointed him *qazi* (judge), and later, 'hospice administrator' – managing charitable institutions. Following another current practice, he had to also assemble many gifts for the sultan to ensure royal patronage: arrows, camels, horses, slaves and other luxuries. But Muhammad bin Tughlaq tended to bestow gifts of far greater value in return on his visitors! This put a strain on the nobility, and in turn on the common people – the peasants and traders – who had to pay taxes to fund this excessive spending!

Batutah described a disastrous famine in 1335 that lasted seven years in which 'thousands upon thousands of people perished of want'. He wrote in detail about Muhammad bin Tughlaq's unpredictable measures as well. He said that in 1327, the sultan forced the inhabitants of Delhi into 'exile'. The sultan, however, felt that Daulatabad was more centrally located and would enable him to manage his growing empire more effectively. The move was carried out rather hastily and peremptorily.

The sultan did make various arrangements to alleviate the sufferings of the travellers. Over the next few years, he had a road constructed between the two distant cities (Delhi and Daulatabad) that was bordered with trees on either side to provide shade. Couriers or messengers who maintained an efficient service of carrying despatches by relays were set up at every *kos* (about two miles), and rest houses were built at successive stages.

Some years later, in 1335, revolts broke out everywhere – the kingdom had become too big to manage centrally – and the sultan revoked his decision and restored Delhi as the capital city. Despite all that Batutah wrote, it is now believed that the old capital was never deserted. There is clear evidence of buildings and other constructive work being carried out in Delhi by Muhammad bin Tughlaq during these very years. It continued to remain a seat of administration and a mint town, with coins being issued from Delhi during 1327–30.

Muhammad bin Tughlaq was also much taken by the dream of foreign conquests. He organized an elaborate expedition into the Himalayan region, or the Qarachal Mountains, which lie between India and China. The troops first captured the city of Jidya in the Himalayan foothills (present-day Kullu–Kangra region). There was just one road that led up to the hilltop and only a single horseman could pass through it at a time. According to Batutah's possibly exaggerated account, very few soldiers made it back.

Still, the consequences of this ill-judged expedition so seriously affected the military strength of the sultan that he could never again collect a large force against his enemies.

Muhammad bin Tughlaq's proposed expeditions to Khorasan (in the west) and the Himalayas were possibly aimed at locating new sources of horses and precious metals. To make up for the shortage of precious metals, Muhammad bin Tughlaq had, in fact, attempted to reduce the weight of his coins and experimented with token money, all of which led to the production of counterfeit coins.

In addition to his other duties, Ibn Batutah was deputed as the sultan's ambassador to the Mongol court in China, and this journey took him as far south as present-day Goa, Honavar in Karnataka, and then Calicut (now Kozhikode), from where he planned to travel on by sea. But the *dhows* (ships) carrying the treasure and gifts meant for Kublai

A ROYAL SECRET!

Muhammad bin Tughlaq was known to be a scholar in several languages, such as Persian, Arabic, Turkish and even Sanskrit. He could dabble equally in maths and philosophy. He rarely asked anyone for advice, and so made the mistakes he did!

Khan, the Mongol ruler, sank. Ibn Batutah dared not return to Delhi to face the sultan's wrath, and left for Morocco.

Muhammad bin Tughlaq, interestingly, was among the first Indian rulers to advance loans (*taccavi*) to the villagers after a devastating famine. He also proposed schemes for improving cropping patterns and extending cultivation. His measures, however, were simply not thought through, and his whims earned him the ire of his nobles and officials. The huge empire that he had built up in the initial years of his reign collapsed by the end of his rule. The governor of Ma'bar, as the Pandyan kingdom was known then, declared its independence. And in the Deccan, the Bahmani Sultanate and the Vijayanagara dynasty emerged as powerful kingdoms in their own right.

Muhammad bin Tughlaq's cousin Firuz Tughlaq, who succeeded him, wrote off the loans granted to the peasants by the former sultan, and helped finance the biggest network of canals known then. The new sultan, who was interested in culture, also commissioned Persian translations (Persian being the court language) of some important Sanskrit texts. He also had an Ashokan Pillar – the one with the mysterious script that was only deciphered 500 years later – placed on the roof of his palace.

The central treasury, however, soon ran dry under Firuz Shah. As Bengal and the southern provinces were lost to the Sultanate, sources of revenue and tribute were fewer. So the import of horses was stopped, and soldiers could no longer be paid on time. Firuz was forced to pick his army from the huge corps of slaves (*mamluks*) from throughout the Sultanate. These soldiers were no match for the cavalry – formed by mounted archers from the regions, north-west of the subcontinent – who came in when Amir Timur invaded in 1398, ten years after Firuz Tughlaq's death.

WHAT AN IMPACT!

No king before him, as records show us, had sent an army towards the Himalayan foothills, and further onto China. No king had so radically issued a new currency in place of the old. But as the consequences show, kings, even as powerful as a Delhi sultan, could not act on a whim. It was a lesson well learnt for future rulers.

MAHMUD GAWAN
The Wazir Who Saved a Kingdom

The most capable ruler of the Bahmani Sultanate was not a king but a wazir – Mahmud Gawan, a nobleman from Persia who had been in the service of three Bahmani sultans for nearly two decades.

The Bahmani Sultanate was founded in 1347 in the Deccan, a century before Mahmud Gawan's arrival. The kingdom came up during a period when the Delhi Sultanate, especially during Muhammad bin Tughlaq's rule, had become too large and unwieldy, and thus, hard to rule. Tughlaq's sudden, ill-thought-out and incomplete reforms, which were reversed just as suddenly, did not help either. Eventually, a revolt by Hasan Gangu, who led a group of rebel nobles against Tughlaq, led to the foundation of the Bahmani Sultanate. Hasan Gangu decided to rule from the newly captured Daulatabad and took the royal, more impressive sounding name of Alauddin Bahman Shah.

Soon after the sultanate's foundation, large numbers of Arabs, Turks, and particularly Persians made their way to the Deccan, drawn by the opportunities of service and quick promotions the new regime offered. These new arrivals – Mahmud Gawan was one of them – were called *afaqis*. Under this new sultanate, they secured several important administrative positions and land grants to match.

The original rebels of the Delhi Sultanate and their descendants, who were the *dakhnis* (Deccanis), resented the rise of the *afaqis*. The *afaqis* also brought with them the knowledge of advanced military technology of the time, such as the use of light firearms and artillery. Later, the addition of the local elite (at times, Hindus) into the ranks of the nobles complicated the situation.

The Bahmani kingdom was at its height when Gawan became wazir. It encompassed quite a large area: most of present-day Maharashtra, south and west Madhya Pradesh, and north Karnataka. For almost all the time it existed, nearly 150 years from 1350 to 1500 CE, the Bahmani kingdom was at war with the rival kingdom of Vijayanagara that bordered it on the south and east. Most of the rivalry revolved around the control of western ports such as present-day Goa where traders from west Asia came. Horses from Arabia were especially needed. The other bone of contention was the Raichur Doab, the fertile ground between the rivers Krishna and Tungabhadra.

The Bahmani Sultanate also fought wars against the kingdom of the region now known as Telangana (centred at Warangal), and the Andhra kingdom to its south. The Reddi kings of the latter kingdom were weak, and both the Bahmani and Vijayanagara Empires wanted to install their own puppet kings, whom they could control easily. Then, in the north, there were the smaller kingdoms of Malwa and Gujarat to be conquered.

To carry out their many military campaigns, the sultanate often relied on the support of chiefs who controlled forts (and land) known as *jagirs*. Such chiefs also contributed soldiers, leading their men in times of war. They would, however, change sides frequently.

Mahmud Gawan emerged as a notable figure in the last years of the reign of Sultan Ahmad II in the early 1460s. There was a rebellion by the sultan's son-in-law, who was supported by the ruler of Malwa. Gawan, who had then just come from Persia, persuaded the rebels to desist and the sultan to pardon them, thereby winning the sultan's goodwill with his superior military strategy.

He would later go on to serve as chief administrator and wazir to three sultans in succession – Humayun Shah, Ahmed Shah III (who died young) and Muhammad Shah II – for over two decades when the Bahmani Sultanate was at its most prosperous. We know this from the account of Afanasi Nikitin, a Russian traveller and horse trader who visited the kingdom and lived there for three years (1469–72 CE).

Under Mahmud Gawan, the Bahmani army successfully annexed a large part of the Konkan coast in the west, including Goa, a vital port. This was then under Vijayanagara control. The Bahmanis assured the safety of merchants and pilgrims (to Arabia) from piratical attacks, and now they also had command over the west coast trade.

In the north, the frontier with Malwa was strictly guarded to prevent any invasions, especially when the Bahmani army was busy elsewhere. In 1470, Gawan worked out an alliance with Vijayanagara that proved effective in defeating Kalinga to the east. A decade later, in 1481, Sultan Muhammad III, with the help of Mahmud Gawan, succeeded in taking Kondapalli in the east Andhra region from Saluva Narasimha, the Vijayanagara general.

Mahmud Gawan encouraged learning, and his madrasa in Bidar, Karnataka, for students to learn Islamic theology, still stands. But his success drew the inevitable jealousy of the older nobles.

According to Afanasi Nikitin, the sultan was a little man, around 20 years old, and maintained a huge army, as did some of the high-ranking nobles. The condition of those who lived in the countryside, such as the farmers, was miserable. The nobles for their part, delighted in luxury. They loved to be carried on their 'silver beds', preceded by some 20 horses decorated in gold, and followed by another entourage of 300 men on horseback and 500 on foot, and behind them were the 'horn-men, ten torchbearers and ten musicians'.

When Mahmud Gawan travelled through the kingdom while on business, he sat on a golden (not silver!) bed, with a silken canopy above, and four horses in gold harness drew his chariot. Around him were crowds of people, and

A ROYAL SECRET!

The Russian traveller Nikitin wrote about Mahmud Gawan. Melikh Tuchar (which is how Nikitin referred to Mahmud Gawan), maintained a huge army of 2,00,000 men. In addition, Gawan's stables held 2,000 horses, and 1,000 of these were always saddled and kept ready for a warrior. His residence was guarded every night by some 100 armed men, 20 trumpeters, and ten torch men; while ten large kettledrums, each attended by two men, were alternately struck throughout the watch.

before him, many singers and dancers, as well as soldiers armed with bare swords, shields, spears, lances, or large straight bows; then there were riders and horses too in full armour. The women who followed on foot carried supplies of water for drinking and washing.

During Nikitin's visit, Gawan apparently spent three years away from Bidar (the Bahmani capital) to curb the chieftains who controlled the highways, and preyed on the traders and merchant caravans.

Gawan's influence on the sultan and his administrative reforms to curb the power of the nobles and chiefs caused much resentment among some. His new system of land valuation had more land coming the royal treasury's way.

The hostility against him grew so much that a group of Deccani nobles presented false evidence to prove Gawan a traitor and convinced Muhammad III to execute him in 1481.

This execution was widely disapproved of. In 1482, the sultan died, of grief (over his error in judgment, the chronicles report) and from thereon began the Bahmani decline. It eventually broke up into five states, with Ahmednagar, Bijapur and Golconda emerging as states constantly battling each other and Vijayanagara as well (the other two states were Bidar and Berar). In 1565, they would team up to defeat Vijayanagara, but within three decades, the Mughal Empire swallowed Ahmednagar. Bijapur and then Golconda being more to the south held on for a while, but were finally defeated by Mughal Emperor Aurangzeb.

WHAT AN IMPACT!

While the Arabs had joined Rashtrakuta service before, now the Persians came in large numbers seeking their fortune. It turned out to be a game-changer in terms of how policies were made, and how court rivalries were shaped. It also resulted in cultural exchanges and adaptations made by Bahmani rulers. The Gol Gumbaz in Bijapur and the Haft Gumbaz of Gulbarga are structures showing Persian and Central Asian influence in their dome and minaret compositions.

KRISHNADEVARAYA
True Glory

Krishnadevaraya (reign: 1509–30 CE), the greatest ruler of the Vijayanagara Empire – belonged to the third dynasty that ruled over the Deccan region. As with the Bahmanis, the Vijayanagara Empire too was formed in the wake of the decline of Delhi Sultanate. Founded in 1336, the Vijayanagara Empire lasted for more than two centuries as a dominant power in south India.

Brothers Harihara and Bukka founded the Vijayanagara Empire when they established the Sangama dynasty in the 14th century. Their dynasty later collapsed as the extended family often fell out with each other, which led to their generals acquiring power. During 1486–1505, the Saluva dynasty ruled in the Vijayanagara Empire, till the emergence of the empire's third dynasty – the Tuluvas, to which Krishnadevaraya belonged.

Right from its beginning, the Vijayanagara Empire built up a great army. They had fine horses from Portuguese traders. The kingdom benefited from trade networks and the presence of trading companies, especially the Portuguese. Krishnadevaraya's army had Portuguese gunners, and the Portuguese helped introduce new armaments into the Vijayanagara army and navy.

Krishnadevaraya's father, Narasa Nayaka, was general to Suluva Narasimha Deva Raya, the last ruler of the Suluva dynasty. After Narasa's death, the throne went to Vira Narasimha, Krishnadevaraya's older brother. Vira Narasimha's rule was short-lived and he died in 1509. It was then that Krishnadevaraya ascended the throne, helped, as the story goes, by his able minister, Timmarasu.

Legend has it that while on his deathbed, Vira Narasimha asked Timmarasu to have his younger brother blinded in order make the throne secure for his own son. Timmarasu, however, had a goat killed, and the animal's eyes were shown to the king who, thus assured, died in peace.

Krishnadevaraya ruled Vijayanagara firmly amid great political and cultural ferment. Besides the Telugu-speaking *nayakas* and other nobles, the kingdom included forest tribes such as the Chenchus in the east, and groups such as the Tulus and the Bearys from the south. Krishnadevaraya's court welcomed talent from all over and extended patronage toward artistic activity of various kinds. He was himself a Telugu poet of some repute.

Like all kings of Vijayanagara, Krishnadevaraya too ruled the capital (that had the same name as the empire) in a well-defended position south of the river Tungabhadra. At that time, it was called Hampi. But the Vijayanagara kings wanted it to reflect their own glory, and hence changed its name to one that meant 'City of Victory'.

Vijayanagara was a symbol of vast power and wealth. Accounts by Portuguese travellers Domingo Pais and Duarte Barbosa paint a vivid picture of a thriving city and kingdom ruled by a capable king, highly respected by everyone. Everyone, including foreign travellers and visitors alike, were impressed by the grandeur of the palace complex and its many temples, such as the Virupaksha Temple, and the elaborate ceremonies of the annual Mahanavami celebrations. At this time, the subordinate kings, the *nayakas* (powerful chiefs who owned land and maintained troops) and other lesser chiefs assembled to pay tribute. Under Vijayanagara rule, temples with features like huge enclosures and entrance gateways (*gopuras*) emerged as major venues to display the state's power, magnificence and influence. Here the kings made offerings to the deity, watched on by a large number kings and ambassadors, especially invited for the occasion.

Under Krishnadevaraya, the kingdom became more powerful than ever before. It was strengthened from within by an administrative structure that had necessary checks and balances. He maintained a well-equipped army, while also relying on the *nayakas*. However, this system worked well when the king was strong. During the reign of a weak ruler, strong *nayakas* could use their territory to build up their own semi-independent holdings (as had happened in the past). As a check, Krishnadevaraya created the rank of lesser chiefs known as *poligars* (or *palaiyakkarars*) in the Vijayanagara service.

Krishnadevaraya recruited wisely. He appointed scholars as administrators and capable people, not just his relatives, as commanders. He hired the Portuguese to command his forts, and Persian mercenary gunners manned the bastions. He recruited foot soldiers from local forest tribes, as well as the finest archers from present-day Odisha – the Denki archers, who were known for their sharp aim.

The king spent the first ten years of his reign establishing his authority over the chiefs and governors, while warding off invasions from Bijapur and Odisha. The conflicts that he faced were the same that had troubled his predecessors: confrontation with the successor Bahmani states (mainly Bijapur and Ahmednagar) over the Raichur Doab, the western ports, and the declining kingdom of Andhra, where the Reddis were now weak. This region was also eyed by the Gajapatis, who ruled trade-rich Odisha at the time, and were a strong power in their own right.

Krishnadevaraya took advantage of differences between his neighbours. When a quarrel broke out between Bijapur and the weak Bahmani ruler, he managed to conquer

A ROYAL SECRET!

In 1524, Krishnadevaraya made his young son his heir, but the boy soon died of poisoning. The king suspected his minister Timmarasu's hand in this heinous act. The loyal and trusted minister and his entire family were punished, and Timmarasu blinded and thrown into prison. Toward the end of his life, however, the minister was released.

both Gulbarga and Bidar, once provinces of the Bahmani kingdom. He conducted a successful campaign southward, and reached as far as Ummattur in present-day Kerala. It became a new province of his kingdom.

From 1513 to 1520, Krishnadevaraya waged regular battles against the Gajapati ruler of Odisha, conquering all his territory up to the river Godavari River, and then raiding as far as the Gajapati capital at Kataka (Cuttack). The king asked for peace, and gave his daughter in marriage to Krishnadevaraya, who consequently, in a related move, returned to Odisha some of the territory he had conquered.

The conflict with Bijapur involved a tug-of-war over the Raichur Fort. While the Vijayanagara king was busy with campaigns in the east, the sultan of Bijapur took advantage of his absence and retook the fort. But Krishnadevaraya soon recovered it with the use of his effective Portuguese gunners. Gulbarga too was raided.

With Krishnadevaraya's death in 1529, the Vijayanagara kingdom's period of great military and administrative success came to an end. The king had nominated his brother Achyuta Raya as his successor, but almost immediately, the latter's chief minister, Rama Raya, rebelled, waged a battle and demanded a share of power. Later, Rama Raya secured all power in his hands.

However, Vijayanagara's might and riches had already made its neighbours very envious. Barely 35 years after Krishnadevaraya's death, the kingdom became an easy target for the Deccan states, who ganged up against his successors, who were busy frittering away their energies on rivalries. The Battle of Talikota in 1565, when the three major Deccani Sultanates – Bijapur, Ahmednagar and Golconda – teamed up against Vijayanagara, dealt a big blow to the kingdom, and it never fully recovered. Rama Raya's brother Tirumala established a new kingdom in the south, but the days of glory never returned.

WHAT AN IMPACT!

Krishnadevaraya was a great administrator, military leader and man of letters. Telugu received a great boost during this time. Hampi became a city admired by travellers and commoners alike. His astute and balanced rule is indelibly associated with Vijayanagara's enduring greatness.

BABUR
Always Up for a Challenge

In 1494 CE, at the very young age of eleven, Babur became king of a small principality of Ferghana (modern-day Uzbekistan) in Central Asia. He was surrounded by hostile relatives eyeing his territory. Yet from the beginning, Babur had a keen desire to prove himself worthy of his ancestors – he was the true heir of both Genghis Khan, the dreaded and admired Mongol conqueror, and Amir Timur, whose invasion in 1398 had sounded the death knell for the Delhi Sultanate.

Babur ruled in north India for only four years (reign: 1526–30 CE), fighting battles all the time, but he would go on to establish the foundations of the mighty Mughal Empire, one that would rule over a big part of the Indian subcontinent like the great dynasties of the Mauryas and the Guptas. Its rulers would make enduring contributions

Babur

in almost every sphere: polity, military strategy, arts and architecture, music and literature.

We learn much of Babur's life and times from his memoirs, the *Baburnama*. Written in his native Chagatai Turki (a Central Asian language) and translated into Persian in the time of his grandson Akbar, the tome eloquently describes the battles he fought in detail and all that he saw in his new home, the plant life in Agra, the weather and the people.

The start to his many victories, however, was not easy. Babur was unlucky in the first few campaigns he waged. He was keen to win Timur's capital of Samarkand for himself, and did indeed secure it, not once but twice. Both times, however, he was ousted, and then he lost Ferghana too. For a while, he wandered the mountains. But he soon recovered, gathered together a small army and captured Kabul. This kingdom, and the region around it, at last gave him a secure base.

At this time, weak dynasties held power in Delhi and Agra. The Sayyids (the fourth dynasty of the Delhi Sultanate) had been followed by the Lodhi dynasty. Under Ibrahim Lodhi, the sultan of Delhi, revenue was erratic, the army weak, and the nobles constantly jostled for power. And so it came to be that Babur, who was in Kabul, received an invitation from two of Ibrahim Lodhi's disgruntled nobles asking him to invade a weakened Delhi, tempting him with the immense riches awaiting him.

The two nobles who wrote to Babur – one was Alauddin, who was Ibrahim Lodhi's uncle; and the other was Daulat Khan Lodhi, the governor of Punjab – believed that Babur, like other invaders, would loot and then return to his own kingdom, thereby leaving the throne free for them. Babur, however, had other intentions. If he secured control over Delhi and Agra, he would finally have a financially secure and large kingdom to rule over.

As they faced each other off at Panipat (now in Haryana), Babur's army was barely one-fourth of Ibrahim Lodhi's huge standing army. But having been on the move since his pre-teen days, Babur was a highly skilled warrior, famed not just for his sharp aim and his skills with the bow, but also for his ability to think on his feet and devise foolproof military strategies for every battle. Two other important aspects that worked for Babur in securing his decisive victories in the four battles that he fought in the Indian subcontinent were his use of firearms (the Lodhi army did not have any field artillery) and his expert deployment of horsemen in ways made popular by Genghis Khan's fabled cavalry.

As the battle began on 20 April 1526, Babur's archers on horseback bypassed the enemy, going around them from the right and left, and then attacked the unwieldy army from the rear. Caught between gunfire and showers of arrows, the Delhi sultan's huge forces were defeated. And within just a few hours, Lodhi and most of his men died on the battlefield.

The spoils revealed by the royal treasuries at Delhi and Agra were immense, and the first business post the triumph was to divide the booty among the troops. It is said that when Humayun, Babur's eldest son, brought his father the glorious diamond known as the famous Kohinoor, Babur returned it to the young prince. His fabled generosity in letting his commanders divide up war spoils among themselves and their soldiers gained him the nickname 'Kalandari', the mendicant friar.

Thereafter, Babur repeated this performance in a far more important battle: the one waged against the Rajputs, who had banded together, accepting the leadership of Rana Sanga of Mewar. Babur knew that the Rana was a rival more formidable than Ibrahim Lodhi. He was rumoured to possess just one eye and one arm and yet had lost none of his courage in battle!

The preparation for this battle in Khanwah (near Bharatpur in Rajasthan) took 25 days. This time, for this important confrontation, Babur made his artillery appear even more menacing by placing dummy wooden guns between the real ones. He also managed to skillfully advance this rigged artillery further ahead while the battle raged. As before, Babur's armies managed to surround the enemy and Rana Sanga was defeated.

Babur fought his next successful battle against the Rajput chief Medini Rai, at Chanderi, and followed it up with his

A ROYAL SECRET!

Babur was an astute observer of nature, as seen from his memoirs, *Tuzk-i-Baburi*. The story also goes that he suspected his enemies of always trying to poison him. Like Chandragupta Maurya, Babur also took in small amounts of poison to make his body habituated to it.

eastern campaign against the Afghans. This specific battle required some improvisation since it involved the presence of the two major rivers of the east – the Ghagra and the Ganga. It seems Babar thrived on crossing rivers and wrote of how he swam across the Ganga in 'thirty-three quick strokes'.

For the battle against the Afghans, Babur had pontoon bridges built to ferry his men and cannons to the other side. Sher Khan, the future Sher Shah Suri, would be among those to offer battle, but he strategically made peace and withdrew. Babur's mobile artillery, which moved on carts, was a striking innovation for India. Big guns had been used before in the siege of fortresses, but light field artillery and muskets were new, and their use gave Babur a decisive advantage over his adversaries. As with his other campaigns, Babur employed deception to confuse the enemy. Some troops were sent across the river by boats to divert the enemy's attention while the artillery was being transported. The result was the collapse of the Afghan rebellion and a treaty of peace was signed with the sultan of Bengal.

Babur returned to Agra for the rainy season. He had found it hot in summer but now he found it delightful, as he wrote. He had wells dug and tanks built beside the river Yamuna, as well as flowerbeds of roses and narcissus planted in gardens. Babur describes in his memoirs the Charbagh he created in Agra, complete with marble pavilions and beds of roses.

Babur's son Humayun took part in the battle of Panipat. During his later campaigns, Babur had, however, sent him to Kabul to hold the fort there. The young prince returned to Delhi when his father fell seriously ill, and then, it is believed, Humayun contracted Babur's illness. As per a legend, Babur circled his son's bed three times, praying that his son's life may be spared in place of his own. This story, of course, has little relation to the fact that Babur, indeed, died a few months after his son's recovery. The king, who had lived a hard life, was only 48 years old.

WHAT AN IMPACT!

It was Babur's repeated failures in west Asia and the loss of his home kingdom there that prompted him to look east towards the Indian subcontinent. The Mughals would make it their base, and Babur's successors would rule as Mughal emperors for over 300 years. Even when their power shrunk, the Mughal emperor was seen as the ruler of all India.

HUMAYUN
Who Lost and Won back a Kingdom

Babur had left no clear succession plans. And so his other sons instantly challenged Humayun (reign: 1530–40 and 1555–56), Babur's oldest and most favoured son, who ascended the throne of Delhi in 1530 CE. Humayun took time to secure control of the kingdom, partly because of his lassitude and partly because of the resistance put up by his stepbrothers Kamran, Askari and Hindal. This distraction was all the time the Afghans, under the brave and capable Sher Khan (later Sher Shah Suri), needed to recuperate and regroup.

In Sher Khan, Humayun had truly met his match. It was during the Bengal campaign that Sher Khan totally outwitted and outmanoeuvred the Mughal emperor. In total control of the roads leading to Bengal, Sher Khan let the Mughal forces occupy Bengal but besieged them on the way back. As Humayun sought to negotiate, Sher Khan

A ROYAL SECRET!

In popular memory, Humayun's life was saved by a water carrier who offered his inflatable sack holding water to the emperor as he swam across the river Ganga to escape Sher Shah Suri's soldiers. History, however, records one of his nobles, Shams al-Din Muhammad, as helping Humayun up the steep banks of the Ganga once he had safely fled the enemy.

went back on his agreement and attacked the Mughals. And in 1539, Humayun lost the throne of Delhi in two battles at Chausa (in modern-day Bihar) and Kannauj. However, he managed to save his life and escape.

Chased out of his Indian empire, Humayun became reduced to a wandering nomad, just as his father had been for a while when young. The dethroned king then made his way north-west, towards Persia, hoping to seek the Shah of Iran's help in recovering his throne. En route, he took refuge in Amarkot in Sindh (now in Pakistan). It was here, during these years in exile, that his son Akbar was born, in 1542.

But Humayun's story was not over yet. He would, in time, recover his throne. In 1555, ten years after the death of Sher Shah Suri, Humayun took advantage of his weaker successors in north India. He advanced from

Kabul with only 15,000 horsemen. He first seized Punjab, defeating Sikandar Suri at Sirhind. As Sikandar was forced to escape towards the Himalayan foothills, Humayun sent his son Akbar in pursuit. He then marched on to Delhi and recaptured it. It seemed as if the Mughal king's luck had turned at last. But nothing ever went well for long with this unfortunate monarch. Scarcely had he enjoyed his throne at Delhi for six months than he slipped down the steps of his palace and died in his forty-ninth year. As a later historian called Stanley Lane-Poole memorably described it, 'He tumbled through life and tumbled out of it'.

It was left to his son Akbar to re-establish and enhance the fortunes of the Mughal Empire.

WHAT AN IMPACT!

Humayun's recovery of the Mughal kingdom after losing it in two successive battles with Sher Shah revealed how the dynasty's fortunes were now tied with this region, i.e., parts of north India that made up the early Mughal empire. West Asia and the north-west, beyond the river Indus, was awash with conflict, where powerful dynasties ruling in Persia and Central Asia constantly battled with each other.

SHER SHAH SURI
A Short yet Magnificent Rule

There are some rulers who may not have ruled for long, but remain highly memorable because of the manner of their rule, the reforms they introduced and the impact of their policies on the common man. Sher Shah Suri (reign: 1538–45 CE) was one such.

Born in Sasaram (in Bihar) in 1484, Farid Khan (as he was known then) was forced to leave home thanks to a constantly nagging stepmother and a weak father. He educated himself in Jaunpur and, in time, took service under Bahlul Khan Lohani, the Mughal governor of Bihar. One day, he saved the ruler from a tiger, fending it off heroically, and so acquired the name Sher Khan (Lion Lord).

After Lohani's death, the governor's young son became suspicious of Sher Khan's growing power and sought the help of Ghiyasuddin Shah of Bengal, who sent his forces to defeat the usurper. Sher Shah defeated them and

Sher Shah Suri

gained complete control over Bihar. But before he could consolidate his position, Babur advanced toward the east and made him capitulate.

His moment came only a few years later, when Humayun ascended the throne. The new Mughal king proved to be no match for Sher Khan's guile and strategy. And so the reign of Sher Shah Suri (from the Suri ethnic group) began.

Sher Shah Suri proved to be an astute ruler. In his financial and other reforms, we see the true origin of many of Akbar's most famous measures. He introduced the silver coin, weighing 178 grains; this was the *rupiah*, on which the later rupee would be based. He also had the land and the expected produce from it assessed, and the revenue due to the state was adjusted to the annual expected price level (which was also now stable).

A ROYAL SECRET!

Sher Shah's coins – the mohur (gold); *rupiah* (silver) and *dam* (copper) – remained in use in Mughal times. The *rupiah* actually had ancient origins, but it was Sher Shah who reformed it, and ensured via its circulation that a uniform currency system prevailed all across his empire.

Sher Shah also had the Grand Trunk Road extended and this greatly helped communications and the postal system. This road dated from Chandragupta Maurya's times but Sher Shah built it further, and the road in his time, reached Rohtas (in central Bihar) and Sonargaon (now in Bangladesh). At a distance of every two *kos* (almost two kilometres), there were *sarais*, with wells. '*Kos* minars' were erected to mark distances. The Purana Qila in Delhi, a very familiar national landmark, was also built during Sher Shah's time.

His brief yet beneficent rule came to an end in 1545, when he was killed by accident in a campaign against the Kalinjar Fort (in present-day Uttar Pradesh), always a difficult bastion to conquer. Various nobles were soon at war with each other. His nephew Adil Shah (or Adali) left all real power in the hands of his Hindu wazir Hemu. Ibrahim Suri, another Afghan noble, seized Delhi and Agra, but Sikandar Suri, another nephew of Sher Shah, took possession of Punjab, and drove Ibrahim out of his new sovereignty.

WHAT AN IMPACT!

There is a note written by Mirza Aziz Khoka, one of Akbar's foster brothers, to Emperor Jahangir, praising Sher Shah for all the steps he had taken. Even Akbar, the Mirza said, followed Sher Shah's revenue directives without changing much.

AKBAR

An Instinctive, Unusual Emperor

Akbar (reign: 1556–1605 CE) was born in Amarkot in Sindh (in Pakistan) in 1542 CE. His father, Humayun, who had lost his throne at Delhi, was at that time out on an expedition accompanied by the king of Amarkot, who had offered him shelter. When the messenger arrived with the news of his son's birth, Humayun rummaged through his own belongings and found a bag of musk that he distributed among his friends, lifting his gaze heavenward in the prayer that his son's fame might one day spread in the world like the fragrance of musk that wafted all around.

As Humayun worked to recover his kingdom, Akbar spent his infancy always on the move, living in camp with his mother, Hamida Banu Begum, by his side. When Akbar was just one year old, his father left him in Kandahar in the care of his uncle, Kamran, who had, however, always bitterly opposed Humayun. When Akbar was five, his

Akbar

vengeful uncle exposed him to shots fired by his father as Humayun's small army laid siege to Kabul. Fortunately, Akbar had a narrow escape.

By the time he was 12 years old, Akbar had acquired considerable skill in riding camels, horses and elephants. He had also gained enough experience in the use of firearms and had seen a lot of warfare as he accompanied his father in his fugitive life. As Humayun prepared to re-enter Punjab in a bid to recover his throne, Akbar was given the responsibility of escorting the womenfolk from Kabul. And then, when he was only thirteen, on his father's unexpected death after having regained Delhi, Akbar was called upon to occupy the Mughal throne. But was the young prince ready for this position?

During the years of Humayun's exile in Persia, Akbar had led a warrior's life and had never learned to read or write. But his sharp memory helped him store an enormous amount of information, and all his life, he remained very curious. The fact that he didn't have a conventional education meant he was never too rigid in his ways; many a time, he rejected traditional or conservative ways of thinking, and he was always keen to discuss new ideas with the people, including those from foreign embassies, who came to his court.

Humayun's trusted adviser and general, Bairam Khan, was Akbar's guardian. It was thanks to Bairam Khan that

Akbar overcame his enemies. But the general was a ruthless man. When Hemu, Adil Shah Suri's trusted general, was defeated and captured during the Second Battle of Panipat in 1556, Bairam Khan insisted that 13-year-old Akbar decapitate or behead the dying prisoner. According to the historian John F. Richards, that year, Panipat saw two successive battles between the Mughal forces and the Afghans led by Hemu. The first battle in October had seen Hemu as victor, following which he declared himself as an independent ruler. Fortunes swung Akbar's way only a month later when the enemies met again at Panipat. This time the Mughals were victorious. Hemu was wounded by a stray arrow and his army scattered in confusion.

Seeing the young king's hesitation at killing a defeated opponent, the general carried out the deed himself. Eventually, Bairam Khan's random acts of cruelty turned Akbar against him. Akbar offered Bairam Khan a choice – accept a position in court, where his wings would be suitably clipped, or leave for a pilgrimage to Mecca. Khan acceded to the latter option but was killed on the way by a personal foe.

Soon, Adham Khan, Akbar's foster mother's son, became too big for his boots. In one of his first campaigns, Adham Khan headed to Malwa where he soundly defeated its ruler, Baz Bahadur. However, instead of sending the spoils to the central treasury, Adham Khan appropriated most of it. Akbar marched against him. Afterwards, Adham Khan murdered Akbar's trusted *vakil* (prime minister), Shamsuddin Ataga Khan. A furious Akbar had Adham Khan thrown down from the ramparts of the Agra Fort, not once but twice, till he was dead.

But this wasn't the last of the immediate enemies Akbar had to quell. He would have to deal with his half-brother, Mirza Hakim, in Kabul, in some years' time, and subdue a group of rebellious nobles called the Uzkegs in the east.

These contentious issues taught Akbar that he had to seek support from other groups. The brave Rajputs, for instance, would make strong, vital allies. On the flip side, a conflict with them would only drain the state of its resources. Akbar also realized that to secure his throne in a land of people with different beliefs and faiths, he had to reach out to its people.

He put in place his Rajput policy by marrying into prominent Rajput families and offering them high positions in the Mughal administrative structure. He married the daughter of the Rajput ruler of Amer (now Jaipur), and subsequently, granted positions of high-ranking nobles in his court to the Amer king's son Bhagwan Das and grandson Man Singh, who served in Akbar's army. Raja Todar Mal, also a prominent noble in the imperial court, came to be associated with the reform of the land revenue system, which involved sending officials into every region to collect data on prices and produce. Akbar did not force his own religion on them. Akbar also abolished the *jizya*, a tax that Islamic rulers used to impose on all their non-Islamic subjects.

Despite these diplomatic initiatives, Akbar had to wage three main battles where he came up against strong and resilient opponents.

Rana Pratap of Mewar was one such worthy foe. Akbar went to war against this powerful Rajput ruler for eight years! In the beginning, however, it was Pratap's father, Rana Udai Singh, who resisted Akbar.

In 1566 CE, a decade into his reign, Akbar led his armies against Udai Singh. As Akbar neared Chittor, the Mewar stronghold from where the Rana ruled, Udai Singh was advised by his loyal officials to retire to the more inaccessible mountainous country. He left a garrison of soldiers in charge of the fort under the command of his able officers, Jayamal and Patta. In October 1567, the fort at Chittor was besieged, and Akbar's skilled workers laid mines to blow up the fort walls.

Then, one night at camp, Akbar happened to spot Jayamal directing the repair of a breach in the fort walls. Aiming accurately, Akbar shot him through his head! As battle commenced, Akbar summoned the Rajputs to surrender.

Udai Singh fled deeper into the hills to Gogunda in Udaipur, a city he had founded a few years earlier. He died in 1572 and was succeeded by his son, Rana Pratap Singh, who remained Akbar's most persistent and determined enemy throughout his life.

Initially, it was Raja Man Singh, at the head of a large army and assisted by Asaf Khan, who undertook an expedition against Rana Pratap Singh. In 1576 CE, the Mughal forces headed to attack the fortress of Gogunda in the Aravalli Hills, but Rana Pratap held guard over the narrow pass of Haldighati that led to Gogunda. At the approach of the imperial army, a fierce hand-to-hand fight began and ended in victory for Akbar. This famous battle of Haldighati led to Rana Pratap losing Gogunda and Udaipur, but the victorious Mughal forces could not capture the Rana.

Later, Rana Pratap was able to recover some of his territory but not the key forts of Chittor and Ajmer. Akbar was, at the time, away in the north-west towards Kabul, where his half-brother Mirza Hakim had laid claim to the Mughal throne. Mirza, however, was forced to cede. Rana Pratap died in 1597, but not before the story of his long and brave resistance became part of legend.

Akbar sent his son, Salim (later Emperor Jahangir), to wage war against Amar Singh, the son and successor of Rana Pratap. It would be Amar Singh who would, in the interests of both kingdoms, make peace with the young prince. The famous forts of Chittor and Ranthambore were taken, and in other campaigns, Kalinjar and Ajmer were occupied. Rajputana retained considerable autonomy as a separate province of the Mughal Empire.

Akbar also took on the Gonds in central India where their brave Rajput warrior queen Durgavati led her armies in battle against Asaf Khan, Akbar's governor of Kara–Manikpur (in present-day Uttar Pradesh). Finally, realizing that further resistance to the Mughal forces was futile, she stabbed herself to death on the battlefield. The small kingdom of Gondwana was overrun and subdued and the royal treasury was plundered.

In 1595, Akbar turned his attention toward the Deccan. In Ahmednagar, Chand Bibi (or Chand Sultana) ruled on behalf of the minor king. She reached an agreement with Akbar, ceding Berar in return for his recognition of the young king. But a rival noble killed her, and fighting broke out amongst the inner factions. The Mughal forces used this as a pretext to invade.

Still, Ahmednagar would resist for some time. In 1600, Akbar advanced upon Ahmednagar and easily occupied Burhanpur, a key town. Prince Daniyal, the Mughal emperor's son, and Abdur Rahim Khan-i-Khana (Bairam Khan's son) attacked Ahmednagar and laid siege to the fort. Soon, the fortress of Ahmednagar was stormed and about 1,500 of the garrison inside met a violent end. However, resistance in the south of this kingdom continued with Malik Ambar, a noble of Ahmednagar, who often used guerrilla tactics against the Mughal forces.

By the late 1590s, with other conquests in Gujarat and Bengal, Akbar ruled over almost the entire Indian subcontinent. During this time, in 1595, he managed to recover Kandahar from the Persians; Humayun had been forced to give up some territory in exchange for the Shah of Persia's promised support to him. The river Helmand now became the western border of Akbar's Mughal

Empire. Kandahar, however, would always remain a bone of contention between the Mughals and the Safavids of Persia (Iran).

Despite the fact that all his conquests had been violent, Akbar wished to rule benevolently. In this, Akbar was very unconventional in his thinking and progressive in his views about different communities living together in harmony. This was perhaps the reason for the introduction of his *Din-i-Ilahi* (Divine Faith): he wanted to establish a unique combination of the best religious and spiritual ideas that appealed to him. Moreover, he wished to prevent sectarian strife by playing the supreme arbiter to resolve all differences, especially related to religion.

Akbar openly opposed the orthodox Islamic scholars (*ulema*) for their outdated thoughts. He also believed in the principle of *sulh-i-kul* (universal civility), where people, regardless of their varying beliefs, would still be decent and civil to one another. Historians have compared this with Ashoka's *dhamma* that had almost similar goals of advocating kindness towards everyone.

After some years, Akbar modified some of Sher Shah's measures. With Raja Todar Mal's able assistance, he had all the land measured. The district revenue officers were instructed to compile data on crops, prices, and revenue collections for a period of ten years. Then, Akbar fixed an average demand, based on the data collected from across his empire, for one decade. In this way, looking at the data he had from all over, he was able to consider regional differences of produce and reach a well-thought-out and careful decision about the annual revenue – taking into account the differences in agricultural productivity all through his empire – that should come to the centre.

This knowledge helped Akbar in his system of classification (*mansab*) of all his military and civil officers. This classification had two strands, where officials were ranked by salary (*zat*), and the size of the cavalry contingents (*sawar*), which the officer had to maintain in keeping with his rank. The system was flexible and allowed for various combinations, such as a high salary with only a small or no cavalry contingent at all in the case of civil officers, for example, accountants and those who managed the imperial household. It also enabled the emperor to move officers from one region to another, to prevent them from creating power centres in one location.

The civil servants or bureaucrats also worked for nobles and other imperial officers. Several of these civil servants or *munshis* were Hindus, such as Chandar Bhan 'Brahmin', who served three later emperors (Jahangir, Shah Jahan and Aurangzeb) and was known for his Persian poetry.

The Mughal princes held the highest positions in the *mansab* system. Akbar appointed each holder (*mansabdar*) of a *mansab* personally. Scholars suggest there must have been almost 4,00,000 horsemen in Mughal service by the end of Akbar's reign. Over time, maintaining such a huge army led to heavy demands being made on the peasantry. Under Akbar's successors, there were too many nobles and not enough land to sustain their salaries. It put a strain on resources, and contributed to the later weakness and decline of the Mughal empire.

The artillery was under Akbar's direct control. He took a great interest in innovations in guns and muskets. When the Portuguese Jesuit missions from Goa visited, the emperor asked them questions about the scientific tools they knew about as well as new developments in artillery.

Akbar's love of learning manifested itself all through his life. Books were compiled and translated from other languages, all under his auspices. The *Akbarnama*, Abul Fazl's book on Akbar, was a detailed account of the customs and traditions of people, besides financial matters, revenue settlements and so on. Equally valuable is the *Ain-i-Akbari*, partly a biography of the emperor and also a minute record of the royal household. The book also has a flattering collection of Akbar's sayings and wisecracks. Akbar maintained a huge library that was, in part, inherited from his father. The *zenana* (imperial harem) had its own well-stocked library too and Gulbadan Begum, Akbar's aunt and Humayun's sister, wrote her brother's memoirs, the *Humayun-nama*.

Faizi, Abul Fazl's equally scholarly brother, and several Hindu scholars translated the 'Nala and Damayanti' episode of the Mahabharata from Sanskrit into Persian. In 1582, Akbar encouraged the translation of the Mahabharata into Persian. The translated version was called *Razmnama* (Book of War).

Akbar also commissioned Badayuni, a respected scholar, to translate the collection of fables called the *Singhasan Battisi* into Persian, with the help of Purushottam, a learned Brahmin. It received the appellation of *Khirad-afza-nama* (the Wisdom-enhancing Book). Badayuni also translated the Ramayana into Persian in 1589. And after four years of hard labour, overseen by Faizi, the *Lilavati* (a treatise on arithmetic), the Bhagavad-Gita and the *Atharvaveda* were rendered into Persian.

In addition to the brothers Faizi and Abul Fazl, the court was blessed with the presence of luminaries like the legendary courtier Birbal, Badayuni and Abdur Rahim Khan-i-Khana (Bairam Khan's son). The latter was an accomplished scholar in several languages, being thoroughly conversant in Persian, Arabic, Sanskrit, Turkish and Brij Bhasha. He composed verses in Brij Bhasha using the pen name Rahim. Raja Todar Mal, known for his work on the revenue system, is also credited with a Persian translation of the *Bhagavata Purana*.

Akbar inherited his interest in painting from his father, Humayun, who had witnessed Persian artists at work during his exile in Tabriz in Persia. When Humayun headed back to Delhi, two Persian artists accompanied him: Abd-al Samad and Mir Sayyid Ali. In Akbar's time, they worked with other artists in the royal atelier.

Among the most prominent painters patronized by Akbar, Mir Sayyid Ali took on the project to illustrate the *Hamzanama*. The illustrations made in this period by

A ROYAL SECRET!

Stories of Birbal and his friendship with Akbar are now the stuff of popular myth. The nobleman's intellectual gifts, uncommon as they were, secured him a place in Akbar's trusted and innermost circle. But Birbal, as Abul Fazl writes in the *Ain-i-Akbari*, was also a musician, a poet, a conversationalist, a storyteller and a jester, all rolled in one. It is said Akbar was devastated when Birbal was killed in the Mughal engagement against the Yusufzais in the north-west in 1585 CE.

Basavan and Govardhan for the *Baburnama* can now be seen in the British Museum.

Akbar had a great ear for music as well. Numerous musicians from Persia, Turan, Kashmir and other places came to the Mughal court. But the most gifted of them all was Tansen, whose matchless voice, as a popular story goes, once caused the skies to open and rain to fall when he sang the raga Miyan Malhar. His tomb in Gwalior, Madhya Pradesh, remains a place of pilgrimage for musicians.

Akbar's buildings, especially those at Fatehpur Sikri, were characterized by a happy blend of several styles. The best that have survived are: Humayun's Tomb, Persian in style and renowned for the simplicity and purity of its design; the magnificent Jama Masjid in Fatehpur Sikri, with its classic Buland Darwaza, the Tomb of Shaikh Salim Chishti and the Palace of Jodhabai; and the Diwan-i-Khas in Akbar's Palace in Agra.

Akbar's last years were difficult owing to the rebellion of his son Salim, later Emperor Jahangir. Two of his sons, Murad and Daniyal, died early on account of excessive drinking. Salim rebelled against his father as he feared Akbar preferred Khusrau, Salim's eldest son. Salim suspected Abul Fazl of influencing his father against him, and had Fazl killed. In 1605, Akbar died from illness, and Salim ascended the Mughal throne.

WHAT AN IMPACT!

Like Ashoka, Akbar sought to make a difference in every aspect of his people's lives. His insistence on civil conduct and goodwill towards all – *sulh-i-kul* – was a recognition of the fact that there were all kinds of people in his kingdom, with different religious beliefs. His political policies and his encouragement of the arts blended elements of Islamic and Hindu traditions to truly reflect the land he ruled over.

JAHANGIR
The 'World Conqueror'

Salim, Emperor Akbar's oldest son, took the title of Jahangir (reign: 1605–27 CE), meaning 'Conqueror of the World.' The first threat to his rule came when his son, Khusrau, rebelled in 1606. The latter had the support of Guru Arjan Dev, who was the fifth guru of the Sikhs. Sikhism was founded in the mid-15th century by Guru Nanak, based on principles of leading a simple life, devotion to one god, and brotherhood among people.

Khusrau's rebellion, however, soon fell apart, and he was compelled to surrender. His supporters were tortured and killed, and Guru Arjan Dev was arrested as well. To demonstrate that the Mughals were the superior power in every way, the guru was tortured and executed. This is seen as an important moment because of which Sikhs became politically active, though their opposition would become more organized in a few more decades in the time of Guru Gobind Singh.

In Jahangir's time, there were frequent naval skirmishes in the Arabian Sea between the Portuguese traders and the British East India Company. During this time, the Portuguese were active on India's west coast and had bases in Goa and the south, in places such as Calicut. The English had come later, but were keen to outwit the Portuguese by sheer duplicity. Their ruse was to get the emperor's attention and secure permanent trading rights, rather than temporary 'farmans' (orders) that came the Portuguese way.

Matters came to a head, and involved a big pilgrim and trade ship called the *Rahimi*, owned by Jahangir's mother, Mariam-uz-Zamani, who came originally from the Rajput state of Amer. First it was captured by the British East India Company as the ship prepared to set off for Arabia, loaded with pilgrims and a cargo of indigo, a product much sought after as a dye. The English levied a heavy fine before letting go the ship. They of course kept the indigo. A couple of years later, around 1611, the Portuguese captured the ship off Arabia, and demanded a heavy ransom and other trading concessions. The capture of a royal-owned ship was like a snub to the Mughals and Jahangir took several punitive measures. Trading privileges accorded to the Portuguese in Surat were withdrawn, their establishments in Daman were forcibly closed, and Portuguese merchants within the Mughal realm were captured and expelled. The

Portuguese had not been as astute as the English, and it was the latter who secured the more advantageous trade privileges from the emperor. As for the ship, it was set afire off the coast of Goa – whether accidentally or deliberately remains a matter of conjecture – and the Portuguese had to compensate the Mughals for this loss.

Elsewhere, Jahangir also continued the policy of conquests. These annexations were based on the twin strands of protection and consolidation. In the north, the fort of Kangra (in Himachal Pradesh now) became part of the empire in 1620 CE. Jahangir also had a strong sense of justice, and implemented certain rules that he hoped would help the common man easily access the emperor in case of need. And so he had a bell hung strategically in the royal palace at Agra; anyone who needed the emperor's attention could pull it. It is said that this bell once drew a donkey's attention, who came by and tugged at the bell repeatedly. For long moments, this caused much consternation and confusion among the court officials!

There were other rules that officials had to obey to ensure that they conducted themselves properly (i.e., didn't ask for bribes or oppress the commoners) and made fair decisions especially when complaints were made against their juniors.

Jahangir inherited Akbar's fine taste in the arts and his love of learning. The artists – Hindus as well as those of Persian origin – who worked in the academy set up by Akbar received greater encouragement during Jahangir's time. The emperor urged them to paint diverse subjects: miniatures, paintings depicting religious and mythological themes, and even animals and birds as well as elaborate scenarios featuring the emperor and his entourage engaged in various tasks such as hunting. Some of this had been seen during Akbar's time, but Jahangir favoured the use of delicate brushwork and the distinct use of perspective that he had seen in European paintings.

Like Akbar, Jahangir was a great collector of manuscripts that he sourced from neighbouring kingdoms including Persia, and of paintings as well. In 1615, a British delegation led by Thomas Roe, presented themselves at Jahangir's court in Agra. Roe would remain for the next three years in Agra as ambassador of the British East India Company. He worked to establish trade relations between the Company and the Mughal empire. After his conversations with the English merchants, Jahangir wished for his own artists to emulate European techniques relating to colour and perspective.

Jahangir wrote his memoirs in elegant Persian. In the *Tuzk-i-Jahangiri* or the *Jahangirnama,* he wrote about events till his seventeenth regnal year, and elaborated his views on aspects of kingship, the kingdom and its provinces, and other facets of courtly life. The latter bits right up to the time of Jahangir's death in 1627 were completed by Mutammad Khan and Mohammad Hadi, scholars in his court.

In the 1620s, as his queen Nur Jahan, her father Itimad-ud-daulah Ghiyas Beg, brother Asaf Jah, and Jahangir's son

A ROYAL SECRET!

Jahangir, or prince Salim, is forever associated in public memory and in the cultural sphere for his fabled romance with Anarkali, a dancing girl in the palace, who captured his heart and earned Akbar's ire. There has been much speculation about Anarkali's identity. A tomb in Lahore is believed to be hers, and Lahore, now in Pakistan, is known for its Anarkali Bazaar. There have been several movie depictions of this love story, including *Anarkali* (1953), a Telugu version (1956), two Malayalam versions (1966 and 2015) and the classic *Mughal-e-Azam* made in 1960, with Prithviraj Kapoor as Akbar, Dilip Kumar as Salim and Madhubala as Anarkali.

Khurram (later Shah Jahan) took over most administrative decisions among themselves – and a rivalry soon developed between Nur Jahan and her stepson, Khurram – Jahangir chose to involve himself more in the arts. As he encouraged his artists to experiment in more genres and styles – and also gave in to his opium habit – it was his very capable wife, Nur Jahan, who took most of the vital decisions relating to administration.

Originally from Persia, her father and brother were soon made members of the Mughal nobility and were granted *mansabs* as recognition of their status. Under Nur Jahan, Persian culture showed its influence in aspects of couture and in culinary synthesis as well. Such adaptations were of course already evident, but Nur Jahan had sophisticated tastes and set high standards with her everyday elegance. Jahangir died in 1627, having ruled for 22 years.

WHAT AN IMPACT!

Jahangir's court rivalled in magnificence the court of the Ottomans of Turkey, and those of other important rulers of the world then, like the Bourbon kings of France, and the Stuarts of England. Scholars, artists, traders and men of religion vied to be at his court that symbolized cosmopolitanism. In his time, the Mughal Empire acquired an aura of wealth, splendour, aesthetic taste and power.

NUR JAHAN
Her Name after the Emperor's

In 1611, six years after his ascension to the Mughal throne, Emperor Jahangir married Nur Jahan. Soon, the new empress became one of the most powerful persons in the empire. It was in the second half of Jahangir's reign (around 1615 or so) that Nur Jahan truly came into her own, wielding great authority over the imperial court.

Nur Jahan's parents came to India from Persia, where her father had fallen on hard times. It was a perilous journey as the caravan made its way from Tehran towards Emperor Akbar's court and, in one instance, bandits attacked the caravan carrying her parents – her father Ghiyas Beg and her mother Asmat Begum who was then pregnant – and three older siblings. The family lost everything except two mules. When the group reached Kandahar, Asmat Begum gave birth to her fourth child, who was named Mehr-un-Nissa (Sun among Women). As the bandits had left them with virtually nothing, her parents decided to abandon the baby girl by the roadside. The caravan leader, Malik Masud, however, was so struck by her beauty that he picked her up and brought her back, returning the newborn to the mother and promising the family that it would never be destitute again.

Nur Jahan

Ghiyas Beg found work at the Mughal court in Agra, where he was first appointed the *diwan* (treasurer) of Kabul, and then, when his good work caught Emperor Akbar's eye, he was moved to Agra and put in charge of maintaining the imperial buildings and mausoleums. His son, Asaf Khan, also became a leading noble in Emperor Shah Jahan's time. In fact, Mumtaz Mahal, whom Shah Jahan was to marry later, was Asaf Khan's daughter. Mehr-un-Nissa was married to a Persian soldier turned nobleman, Sher Afghan, who had also been in Jahangir's (then Prince Salim) service once. She had a child from this marriage: a daughter called Ladli Begum.

After her husband died in a shooting accident in 1607, Mehr-un-Nissa was taken in as a lady-in-waiting by the royal harem (*zenana*) in Agra. In the spring of 1611, the young woman met Emperor Jahangir at a palace bazaar. The two were married a few months later.

Soon after this, Jahangir in his memoir, *Tuzuk-i-Jahangiri*, noted how impressed he was with her superb marksmanship with the musket. He wrote of how Nur Jahan felled a tiger with her very first shot. He first gave her the title 'Nur Mahal' and then 'Nur Jahan'.

After a few years, as Jahangir's health diminished and he became more interested in encouraging miniature painting and writing his memoirs, Nur Jahan began taking over some of the court's administrative tasks. In most of this, however, she always consulted Jahangir. Nur Jahan's family already held high positions in the Mughal court, and her assumption of authority was, of course, resented by many, including old-timers and nobles such as Mahabat Khan and her stepson, Prince Khurram.

Nur Jahan's political accomplishments as empress are well documented. Her first act, very unusual for that time, was to add her own name, 'Nur Jahan, the Queen Begum', to the emperor's signature in all official letters, farmans (orders) and grants of appointment. This meant she had a say in promotions and demotions in the *mansabdari* service. Soon she started holding an informal court of her own, where she passed judgment on matters.

She took a special interest in the condition of women. Her favourite cause was to provide sufficient dowries for the marriages of orphan girls, who had been captured in war and sent to the harem as maids.

The empress also had coins struck in her name; this step by Nur Jahan was an unparalleled one in Indian history. She also traded with European merchants and ensured that duties collected from travelling merchants reached the royal treasury, rather than being claimed by middlemen. Foreign emissaries at the Mughal court chose to present their credentials to her. She also reached out to highly-placed women in other countries such as the queen mother in the kingdom of Turan (in Central Asia).

Moreover, historians have also recorded her valiant efforts at quelling a rebellion against her husband. In 1626 or so, Mahabat Khan, the disgruntled general, rebelled. He chose his moment well. It was when Jahangir was on his way back from Kabul and was stranded on the banks of the river Ravi in Lahore. Nur Jahan, who was accompanying the emperor, negotiated a way out by an elaborate game of deception and cunning. At first, she attempted an escape and rode out to battle on an elephant, but was compelled to surrender. She was surrounded by the many Rajput troops loyal to Mahabat Khan – in this period of around 100 days, he was effectively 'emperor'. But Nur Jahan broke the rebel leader down in a knotty plot of deceit by making him believe he had Jahangir's support.

Soon, Mahabat Khan had lost most of his supporters and was compelled to escape towards the Deccan. Prince Khurram who had rebelled against his father in 1622 but reconciled with him in 1626, now advised Mahabat Khan to seek Jahangir's forgiveness. But Jahangir was to die only a year later, in October 1627, at Lahore.

At this, a war of succession broke out. Nur Jahan made attempts to have her son-in-law, Shahryar (Ladli Begum's husband and Prince Khurram's younger brother), crowned the next emperor. But Khurram acted fast. He sent messages to Nur Jahan's brother, Asaf Khan, who was his father-in-law, ordering that all possible rivals be put to death. Asaf and his men killed at least four claimants to the throne, including Nur Jahan's son-in-law Shahryar.

In 1628, Prince Khurram took the throne as Emperor Shah Jahan. Asaf Khan was rewarded with the position of chief minister, and Nur Jahan was sent to a dignified exile in Lahore, where she lived for the next 18 years with her daughter, Ladli Begum, whose husband Shahryar had been killed in the war of succession. She died in Lahore on 18 December 1645. After a modest funeral, she was buried in a tomb she had designed herself.

Shah Jahan made attempts to erase her public presence, such as destroying coins that had her image along with Jahangir, but Nur Jahan's vivid and eventful life made the former empress not just unforgettable but also a popular queen in history.

Her political manoeuvrings notwithstanding, Nur Jahan left an indelible mark on art, architecture, fashion and poetry. Her architectural contributions are seen in buildings with a fusion of Persian and Indian styles.

Built in 1622, her father's mausoleum in Agra is regarded as a forerunner to the Taj Mahal. A beautiful garden–tomb of Mughal India, it is the first example of inlaid marble work in a style adapted from the Persian tile-mosaics. The monument has detailed latticework, with semi-precious stones embedded on the walls. Although Jahangir had

A ROYAL SECRET!

Nur Jahan was quite the fashion icon! When she came to Agra first to live in the palace as a handmaiden, she endeared herself with her skills in embroidery and dress designing. She made popular the tight salwar, and the use of delicate muslin and embroidered gold thread in *odhni*s (scarves). The longer skirt lengths she preferred soon became popular, and she also introduced new ways of designing jewellery.

commenced building his tomb while he lived in Lahore, it was Nur Jahan who completed the marble structure after his death. Her influence is evident in the dainty marble inlay work, and her love of nature is visible in the delicate floral patterns on buildings.

While Jahangir's gardens in Kashmir, such as the Shalimar Bagh, are breathtaking, so too are Nur Jahan's gardens, such as the Noor Afshan (Light Scattering) in Agra, completed around 1619. Other splendid gardens include the Noor Manzil (Abode of Light) and Moti Bagh (Garden of Pearls) in Agra, and the Shah Dara (Royal Threshold) around Jahangir's tomb in Lahore. All these gardens had flowers, fruit trees and vines, and fountains and pavilions.

Nur Jahan was also known for her poetry, for she was well versed in Arabic and Persian. She wrote under the name of Makhfi (the concealed one), though this was a pen name adopted by some other royal women, such as Salima Begum (Bairam Khan's widow, who later married Akbar), and Zeb-un-Nissa, Aurangzeb's daughter. Nur Jahan's poetry shows glimpses of her spontaneity and wit.

The empress also ordered the construction of inns (*sarais*) at regular intervals along the roads. These also offered resting places for horses. Some even had gardens.

Nur Jahan's patronage extended to painting too, which was one of Jahangir's passions as well. Ustad Mansur, from this period, is known for his depictions of birds, including the now-extinct dodo, and the Siberian crane. During their reign, miniature painting became a high art form.

WHAT AN IMPACT!

As a ruler alongside Jahangir, Nur Jahan was decisive, forthright and effective. Her interventions ensured that the Mughal empire dominated not just politically but culturally as well. The gardens and mausoleums built under her set new standards in taste and excellence. Several artistic innovations she helped introduce, such as inlay work and engravings on marble, featured in later Mughal buildings, most notably in the Taj Mahal.

SHAH JAHAN
A Life of Mastery and Misery

The honorific title of Shah Jahan (King of the World) was given to Prince Khurram by his father, Emperor Jahangir, after the young prince had returned victoriously from the Deccan, following his conquest of Ahmednagar. Later, the young prince would rebel against his father, suspecting that the queen Nur Jahan was working against him.

Shah Jahan ascended the throne in 1627. The ambitious young emperor was a masterful military strategist, and a lover and patron of the arts as well. During his time, some of the most beautiful buildings of the Mughal period came up: the Red Fort (in Delhi) and the Taj Mahal (in Agra) – the mausoleum of his wife Mumtaz Mahal – both featuring a wonderful blend of Persian and Indian styles.

As prince, Shah Jahan had never quite trusted Nur Jahan. In 1622, during Jahangir's reign, Nur Jahan ordered

Shah Jahan, with his sons: Dara Shikoh, Shah Shuja and Aurangzeb (and an uncle)

Khurram to march to Kandahar against the Persians who had besieged the city. The young prince refused. He believed the queen would use his absence to influence his father and name her son-in-law Shahryar as the emperor's heir. Instead, he gathered an army, and marched against his father and the queen.

However, Khurram's rebellion was unsuccessful, and over the next four years, till 1626, the defeated prince first sought shelter in Mewar, and then fled to the Deccan. He was forced to depend on the support of the sultan of Golconda and Mewar to the north, and Persia's Shah Abbas, to whom he had surrendered Kandahar.

Around this time Asaf Khan, his step-uncle and father-in-law, handed over Shah Jahan's imprisoned elder brother, Prince Khusrau, to him. Khusrau was then killed on Shah Jahan's orders. It was the first in a series of executions that Shah Jahan would carry out, especially after Jahangir's death in 1627. Helped by Asaf Khan, Shah Jahan's brothers and nephews were all put to death.

There is no doubt that Shah Jahan could be cruel – a trait almost considered necessary at the time for a monarch to emerge triumphant. Yet he could sink into deep misery at the loss of the people he loved deeply – for instance, when he lost his beloved wife, Mumtaz Mahal, and when his cherished daughter, Jahanara, suffered severe burn injuries. It is reported that Shah Jahan watched over Jahanara devotedly, monitoring her progress on a daily basis and sitting at her bedside for long hours.

As prince, Shah Jahan was a victorious military commander, but as emperor, his campaigns were not so successful. Shah Jahan was never able to recover Kandahar, much treasured by the Mughals as it linked them with places associated with their past: Kabul and Ferghana. Shah Jahan wanted to recover Kandahar as that would help secure another old Mughal dream: the recovery of Samarkand – a city made famous by Amir Timur, an ancestor of Emperor Babur, the founder of the Mughal Empire – farther up north.

As emperor, Shah Jahan (reign: 1628–58 CE) resorted to diplomacy to deprive the Persians of Kandahar, while managing to retain their loyalty as an ally. But the Persians turned the tables quietly. They pretended to support the Mughal army commanded by Prince Aurangzeb, Shah Jahan's third son, when he led a campaign against the Uzbeks in Central Asia. The Persians then took advantage of Aurangzeb's advance on Balkh and recaptured Kandahar. Faced with a terrible winter and a tired army, Aurangzeb was unable to recapture Kandahar. He could not retain Balkh either.

Shah Jahan once again tried to recover Kandahar with a military campaign led by Dara Shikoh, his oldest son. The siege lasted five months, but the Mughal artillery just couldn't make a dent in the fort's ramparts. The weaknesses

A ROYAL SECRET!

Shah Jahan was especially close to his eldest child, his daughter, Jahanara Begum. At seventeen, she took over the duties and responsibilities of chief queen or empress when her mother, Mumtaz Mahal, died. She was known to be very learned, having access to the library at Agra, first set up by Akbar. Jahanara was known to be generous and pious, and she had a sharp political sense.

She had several buildings commissioned; Chandni Chowk in Old Delhi owes much to Jahanara.

of the Mughal army – its inability to hold prolonged sieges – had been exposed.

These failed campaigns served as a good lesson for Aurangzeb, who turned his attention to southern India and gave up all vain ambitions to go north once he ascended the throne. As per established precedent, he rebelled against his father – and this fight for the Mughal throne was a brutal, vicious contest among all of Shah Jahan's sons.

In 1656, as rumours of Shah Jahan's illness spread, Aurangzeb was quick to act. Winning crucial battles against his brothers, he had his father imprisoned in Agra Fort. It is here that Emperor Shah Jahan was cared for by his oldest daughter, Jahanara Begum, till he died almost a decade later.

It is said that during his days of confinement, Shah Jahan often looked forlornly across at the Taj Mahal, the mausoleum he had built in memory of Mumtaz Mahal, who was his most beloved wife, and who was buried there. Mumtaz was Nur Jahan's niece and Asaf Khan's daughter, and Shah Jahan sought Mumtaz's advice on many an occasion, and she accompanied him on several campaigns.

When Mumtaz Mahal died during childbirth in 1631, Shah Jahan was inconsolable. It was then that he decided to build a magnificent mausoleum in her honour. Today, the Taj Mahal is the most visited and photographed monument in India and seen as an enduring symbol of love. In 1983, the Taj Mahal was declared a UNESCO World Heritage Site. And it is because of this everlasting legacy that Shah Jahan remains the greatest builder among the Mughals.

WHAT AN IMPACT!

Shah Jahan's buildings at Agra and Shahjahanabad have made him immortal. While the world knows about the Taj Mahal, the Red Fort in Shahjahan's capital of Shahjahanabad, in Delhi, has enduring significance in India's present. Built of impressive red sandstone amidst sprawling grounds, it is from the Red Fort (Lal Qila) that India's prime ministers address the nation every Independence Day on 15 August.

AURANGZEB
Failing to Hold Things Together

Aurangzeb (reign: 1658–1707 CE), the longest-reigning Mughal emperor, seized the throne in a most brutal war of succession. It all began when Shah Jahan fell ill in 1656. Dara Shikoh, his eldest and most favoured son, remained in Shahjahanabad (now Old Delhi). The other three brothers, who had been appointed viceroys of different provinces, rebelled. They feared that the real news – the death of the emperor – was being hidden to preempt Dara Shikoh's elevation to the throne.

It was Shah Shuja (Shah Jahan's second son) who first declared a rebellion in Bengal, forcing Dara Shikoh to send the imperial armies against him. Aurangzeb (Shah Jahan's third son), meanwhile, cannily joined forces with Murad Baksh (Shah Jahan's youngest son), and they took on the imperial armies, now overstretched on two fronts, at Samugarh (near Agra). The imperial armies were defeated and when Dara tried to reach out to other nobles for help, he found that Aurangzeb had already bribed the *mansabdars* and other high-ranking officials.

Finding himself trapped, Dara left Shahjahanabad and headed north-west, desperately seeking support. He moved from Lahore to Kathiawar and thereon to Sindh, where an Afghan chief betrayed him, handing over Dara to Aurangzeb's pursuing army. Dara was brought back to Delhi, where he was paraded in rags. And, one night in August 1659, four men, sent on Aurangzeb's orders, murdered him.

Of the two other claimants to the throne, Shah Shuja had fled the country, while Murad Baksh had been imprisoned (he was later executed). What a bloody end! Now, finally, Aurangzeb felt secure.

In the five decades of Aurangzeb's reign, the Mughal Empire expanded so much that it could hardly be ruled any longer! His empire stretched far to the south, almost reaching to the borders of present-day Tamil Nadu; it extended to the east, and included parts of Assam. Areas of present-day Pakistan and even southern Afghanistan were part of it.

Aurangzeb spent most of his years of rule in the Deccan. During this time, he conquered the Deccan sultanates – the successor states of the large realm of the Bahmani sultans. His base would be a city that would come to bear his name, Aurangabad (in Maharashtra), in northern Deccan, just a few miles away from Tughlaq's Daulatabad.

In some fairness to Aurangzeb, taking control of the Deccan was essential as it was immensely trade-rich, and its ports linked south Asia with ports of Southeast and west Asia, and then Europe. Moreover, the disparate kingdoms of the Deccan made for an easy contest for the Mughal Empire.

However, conquering the Deccan and taking on the different kingdoms – chiefly Bijapur and Golconda – was an entirely different story. Aurangzeb hadn't bargained for the very astute Shivaji and his quick-moving horsemen, who, despite their smaller numbers as compared to the Mughal armies, were at ease in the ravines and hilly terrain of the Deccan. Annexing the Deccan states took guile and patience, and it meant that experienced Mughal commanders, such as the Rajput Raja Jai Singh, had to spend years in negotiating and manoeuvring their way past the armies of Bijapur and Golconda, isolating Shivaji in the process, to ensure their final annexation.

Once these southern conquests were accomplished, Aurangzeb tried integrating the ruling classes of these states into the *mansabdari* system. The Mughal state just could not bear the additional load of these new officials. In the early part of Aurangzeb's reign, as historians have calculated, there were 191 officers holding ranks from 2,000 to 7,000 (i.e., they had to maintain these many horsemen for the Mughal army); 32 of them were from the Deccan. In the second half of his rule, the number of officers of the highest rank had increased to 270; 95 of them came from the Deccan. It was all too top-heavy!

The newly conquered areas of the Deccan in Aurangzeb's time yielded much less revenue when compared to the fertile plains of the north. More crucially, this region had suffered a devastating famine during Shah Jahan's reign. And so there was no increase in resources, making life hard for several of Aurangzeb's *mansabdars*.

From the manner he treated his allies, especially long-standing political allies such as the Rajputs, it would appear that Aurangzeb was just unable to get on with people. In a manner quite like Tughlaq again, he alienated them when he needed their support the most.

For instance, Aurangzeb sent his troops into Jodhpur, the chief city of Marwar, when its ruler Jaswant Singh, an ally of Aurangzeb against Dara Shikoh, died in Kabul, fighting on behalf of the Mughal Empire.

A trusted noble of Jaswant Singh called Durgadas Rathor had journeyed to Shahjahanabad with the two queens, who had subsequently given birth to two boys. Ajit Singh was the older and hence the rightful heir to the throne of Marwar. But Aurangzeb had already appointed Jaswant Singh's nephew as administrator of the region. This was a first step to acquiring Marwar as a *jagir*, bringing it directly under Mughal rule.

Aurangzeb imposed strange and harsh conditions, such as leaving Ajit Singh (along with the queens) in

Shahjahanabad to be brought up in the imperial harem in accordance with Islamic customs. This was just unthinkable for the Marwar entourage, and Durgadas Rathor contrived to ensure the family's escape from Shahjahanabad, all disguised as men and young boys. Marwar was placed under a Mughal governor, but the soldiers loyal to the old king fought on sporadically from the hills.

Another escape from the Mughal court, this time in Agra, has, of course, acquired the status of a legend. It is about how Shivaji and his son, Sambhaji, escaped from the chambers where they had been confined, after Shivaji had stood proudly defiant against Aurangzeb's behaviour in court.

The Rajputs, and specifically the family of Jai Singh, including his son Ram Singh, paid the price for Aurangzeb's wrath, as Shivaji had been under their protection. Some of Ram Singh's lands were confiscated, and he was sent to fight the Ahom forces in the east, to recover Guwahati (in Kamarupa, present-day Assam).

Ram Singh, moreover, was not able to overcome the impressive stand taken by the Ahom commander, Lachit Borphukan. This confrontation, known as the Battle of Saraighat, took place on the river Brahmaputra and is one of medieval India's best-known naval battles. The mighty Mughal army, faced by a determined Borphukan with a much smaller force, was forced to withdraw.

Some scholars refer to Aurangzeb's bigotry in reinstituting the *jizya*, a tax paid by non-Muslims, as a

A ROYAL SECRET!

Historians have suggested that the many revolts against the Mughals in Aurangzeb's time were facilitated by the spread of light firearms. Even the village blacksmith could churn out small firearms; and even a peasant could easily learn to shoot with them. The peasants suffered due to the heavy taxation (with little state investment in return), and when it got too much, they at times seized their firearms and revolted. The hordes of armed peasants who roamed the countryside threatening royal convoys – posed as great a threat to the Mughals as the swift, horse-borne Maratha warriors.

sign of his becoming a 'hardliner', or a fanatic. On the other hand, it could have been a political strategy: to help him reach out to his own base of conservative supporters and ensure more revenue to the royal coffers, for Aurangzeb's military campaigns had proved a drain on the treasury.

At the same time, it is a well-recorded fact that Aurangzeb did ensure the protection of some temples and Jain monuments, and he continued the practice of giving land grants to learned Hindu scholars in Guwahati, Benares, Khandesh and elsewhere. For example, in 1680, Aurangzeb gave orders that his officials were not to harass a Hindu ascetic called Bhagwant Gosain, who lived in Benaras.

The last few decades of Aurangzeb's reign were marked by rebellions all through the empire. The harshness of Aurangzeb's policies led to the breakout of more and more revolts, most often led by the zamindars. Initially, these were isolated events; in time, however, a kind of unity emerged among the various groups. For example, ties of kinship like those between the Jats, or religious solidarity like that binding the Sikhs, especially after the execution of Guru Hargobind – served as common bonds that united the protestors.

In 1707, Aurangzeb died at the age of eighty-nine. His modest tomb is located on the roadside near the city of Aurangabad. In striking contrast to his predecessors, he shunned all pomp and splendour.

WHAT AN IMPACT!

Aurangzeb's long campaign in the Deccan was a sign that the Mughal empire was overstretched and much too centralized. It was hard to sustain such an empire, with its large numbers of nobles and soldiers. It is little wonder that the empire collapsed soon after Aurangzeb.

DURGAVATI
A Queen's Resistance

Rani Durgavati's brave fight against Akbar, the powerful Mughal emperor, remains the stuff of legend. It was a battle unequal in every way, but her resistance is a story of heroism, dignity and 'honourable' defeat.

Gondwana was a small kingdom in central India. It included parts of present-day eastern Madhya Pradesh, Chhattisgarh and north-western Odisha. Centred around Jabalpur, it had existed from the 12th century onward, successfully able to stave off enemies as it was located in a thickly forested region, in the rocky and rugged Deccan plateau.

Durgavati was born in 1524, the daughter of Keerat Rai, who ruled over the neighbouring kingdom of Banda in western Uttar Pradesh. In 1542, she was married to Dalpat Shah, the son of Sangram Shah of Gondwana. Soon after, a son, Vir Narayan was born in 1545.

A ROYAL SECRET!

The Rani Durgavati Vishwavidyalaya, as the University of Jabalpur, Madhya Pradesh, is now called, was renamed in her honour. The train from Jabalpur to Jammu is also called the Durgavati Express.

Dalpat Shah, however, died five years later, and Durgavati became regent for her young son. She ruled with the help of two loyal officials called Man Thakur and Adhar Simha. These men came from different castes, an indication that Durgavati was able to balance different political forces in her court. In the 1550s, the Mughals had reconquered Delhi and Agra, but the Afghans were strong in the east, and the kingdom of Malwa in the west was equally powerful.

Durgavati was able to beat off an attack by Baz Bahadur, who had become king of Malwa in 1556. But things changed in 1562, once the Mughal Emperor Akbar began conquering kingdoms to the west and south of Delhi and Agra. After Malwa was conquered in 1562, Akbar sent feelers to Durgavati, but she refused to accept Mughal suzerainty, for this meant the payment of tribute and other revenues.

The first battle between Gondwana's forces and the bigger Mughal army happened at Narrai in 1564, a place where the river Gaur met the river Narmada. Soon after her army commander Arjun was killed, Durgavati took over the command of her army. That first day of battle, the two sides were equally matched. But on the second day, the Mughal army fielded its immense barrage of artillery while the armaments on the Gond side were comparatively rudimentary. During this battle, Durgavati's son, Vir Narayan, sustained lethal injuries and could fight no longer.

Seated high on Sarman, her war elephant, Durgavati continued fighting till she was struck by arrows. One rendered her briefly unconscious. Her army panicked and scattered in disarray. But rather than surrender, Durgavati, when she came to, preferred death to humiliation. She stabbed herself on 24 June, a day that is still marked as 'Rani Durgavati *balidan divas* (day of sacrifice)'.

WHAT AN IMPACT!

There have been few warrior queens in history and Rani Durgavati's place among them is assured. Durgavati's resistance was among several things that convinced Akbar how important it was to reach out to adversaries, make them one's allies and treat them with dignity, instead of spending state resources on long, unending struggles.

SHIVAJI

The Challenger Who Made His Own Rules

As the Mughal dynasty, from the 1640s onward, tried to establish control over the Bijapur and Golconda sultanates in the Deccan, a formidable group emerged – the Marathas. Under the leadership of the very able and sharp-witted Shivaji, this peasant–warrior group soon became a huge thorn in the Mughals' side. He was swift, employed guerrilla tactics – a series of swift, plundering attacks made possible through his knowledge of the rocky Deccan terrain – very effectively, and his hold over forts meant he could inflict a quick attack and melt away in the hills just as quickly.

Shivaji (reign: 1674–80 CE) was born in 1630 in the hill-fort of Shivneri, north of present-day Pune district in Maharashtra. He was the second son of Shahaji Bhonsle and Jijabai. Shahaji had served many masters as a military general. He had his own *jagir*, and added to it from the grants he was given in service. Shahaji began his career in the service of the sultan of Ahmednagar; he then served the Mughals for a while, and later returned to Ahmednagar. When he died in 1664, during a hunting expedition with his son, Shivaji, he was in the service of Bijapur.

Shivaji defies Aurangzeb

Shivaji grew up in Pune and, in time, came to know the rugged terrain well. His education included reading and writing, riding, and warrior skills such as fencing, archery and wrestling. Besides his mother, Jijabai, he was mentored by Dadaji Kondev, the *jagir*'s trusted administrator. This region had seen much devastation following years of warfare and a famine in the very year of Shivaji's birth. When Kondev died in 1647, Shivaji, who was then around seventeen years old, took charge of the administration.

One of his first small conquests was the capture of the hill-fort of Sinhagad, which overlooked Pune. Shivaji soon figured out that the best way to control this region was to establish a hold over the forts located at strategic places. This was possible by bringing together an army of horsemen who could ride fast and furiously through the ravines and passes of the Deccan. It is here that the image forever associated with him – Shivaji leading a band of horsemen, towards a hill-fort, their swords raised high – was formed.

With his early conquests, Shivaji directly challenged the Bijapur Sultanate. Shivaji captured the Torna Fort (in

Pune district). He and his men thus came into possession of revenue collections from trade and the nearby villages. Shivaji then built a new fort east of Torna, right on the hill slopes, and called it Raigad. It would serve as his base for some years.

Between the years 1650 and 1655, Shivaji persuaded many *deshmukhs* (landholders) and soldiers to join him. He also began the construction of another fort in the region – Pratapgad – that was completed in 1656. That same year, he turned his attention south and conquered new areas. Soon, Shivaji had control of eight important passes, from where travellers, armies, and others moved through the Western Ghats along the Konkan (west coast).

The Bijapur Sultanate did not react immediately. Its ruler then, Mohammad Adil Shah, was severely ill, and Bijapur itself was under attack from the Mughal armies led by Prince Aurangzeb, son of Emperor Shah Jahan. Things, however, shifted suddenly in the year 1656. Aurangzeb, in charge of the Deccan, left hurriedly for Agra, as rumours of Shah Jahan's illness spread throughout the empire and beyond.

Taking advantage of this uncertainty, Shivaji made more conquests. His campaigns took him north of the Konkan to raid and capture the towns of Kalyan and Bhiwandi, besides the fort of Mahuli (near Thane, Mumbai). These territories had been given over to the Mughals by Bijapur.

By 1659, Shivaji's conquests had drawn much attention. Bijapur, under a new sultan – the 18-year-old Ali Adil

Shah II – knew it had to act. The final provocation came when Shivaji successfully beat back the Bijapur army near Purandar Fort on the Konkan coast. Finally taking action, Bijapur sent one of its ablest and most reputed commanders, Afzal Khan, to deal with Shivaji.

Afzal Khan led a big army of around 10,000 soldiers into the Western Ghats. Shivaji had holed himself up in Pratapgad Fort (south of Pune). It was an astute move as Afzal Khan's army, like all armies of big states, was more suited to fighting on wide-open plains. They had a huge number of foot soldiers, horsemen, elephants, cannons, and siege-breaking equipment, such as battering rams, but all this did not allow for fighting in the narrow ravines and steep hillsides of the Deccan.

Shivaji too knew his limitations. His men could manage skirmishes on the mountain passes and quick raids, but open warfare against a far bigger army was a challenge. So, as Afzal Khan spread his forces around Pratapgad Fort, with Shivaji inside, both sides played a waiting game, for five months through the monsoons.

Eventually, negotiations between their advisers led to the two men agreeing to a meeting. Both men suspected duplicity. And so both Afzal Khan and Shivaji were secretly armed. Shivaji wore metal armour under his clothes and a skull-protector sheathed by his turban. He had a hidden dagger that he could reach with one hand, and on the fingers of the other, he sported sharpened iron claws. Afzal Khan had his own dagger. Stories vary on who struck the first blow. In any case, the two men fought, or as another version goes, pretended to reach each other in an embrace. And Shivaji's iron claws tore apart Afzal Khan. Following this, his men fell on Afzal Khan's soldiers.

Shivaji's victory over Afzal Khan emboldened him more. He made new raids down south and east toward Satara and into present-day north Karnataka. He also managed to secure the large and very important fort of Panhala, near Kolhapur in today's central Maharashtra.

In 1660, Bijapur once again sent its army to tackle Shivaji, this time under the leadership of the shrewd and cunning Sidi Jauhar. The Bijapur army effectively trapped Shivaji inside Panhala Fort. But one night, Shivaji pulled off yet another daring escape.

As the story goes, in the depths of the night, the Maratha leader and his men left the fort to make their way to Vishalgad Fort. A small band led by Shivaji's loyal commander, Baji Prabhu Deshpande, and a Shivaji look-alike called Shiva Nhavi, remained behind to deliberately deceive the enemy and later, for the escape was bound to be discovered, to hold off the pursuing army in a narrow mountain pass. Though Shivaji lost a great many men in this battle, including his trusted commander and Shiva Nhavi, he made it to Vishalgad Fort, which he easily captured.

During this period, Shivaji set about building up a small naval fleet, made up of fast-moving and small sailing boats.

Despite his defiant show against Bijapur, Shivaji knew that the Mughals posed a far greater challenge. This became especially threatening around 1665 when, with Aurangzeb now secure on the throne, the Mughal state turned its attention towards the Deccan once again.

In early 1660, when Shivaji was fresh with new conquests, Shaista Khan, a Mughal commander and Aurangzeb's uncle, advanced with his army and seized the districts that had once been part of Ahmednagar, and other areas on the north Konkan coast. The Mughal army also devastated crops and fields around Shivaji's home *jagir* around Pune. For three years, the Mughal armies held the upper hand and then Shivaji pulled off yet another daring raid. In the April of 1663, Shivaji and his men entered Pune dressed as a wedding party! Some of his other soldiers entered the city as well, disguised as helpers, porters and labourers.

They bided their time and, as night fell and the Mughal army camping within the city's walls went to sleep, they carried out a bold night strike. Shaista Khan himself was attacked and, as is believed, lost some fingers of his hand before he escaped; his son, however, perished in the attack, and several more soldiers were killed before Shivaji and his men vanished into the darkness yet again.

When told of the incident, a furious Aurangzeb forthwith transferred Shaista Khan to Bengal. But Shivaji wasn't done yet. One year later, in 1664, Shivaji raided the trade-rich port of Surat, the main port for the Mughal Empire. The emperor, the women of the royal palace, and many nobles owned and invested in cargo ships that frequented the port, and traded in cloth, opium, tin and fine goods; it was also a port for transporting pilgrims to the city of Mecca in Arabia. Shivaji captured a huge booty, and devastated large parts of the city.

The Mughal army sent against Shivaji this time was huge and led by Raja Jai Singh, the Rana of Mewar. Shivaji knew he was up against a tough and clever opponent.

Using tried and tested tactics, Jai Singh burned the countryside around Pune to deprive Shivaji and his men of supplies. Jai Singh also sent messages to Bijapur to ensure that the latter did not ally with Shivaji. As Jai Singh systematically set about taking on Shivaji's forts, one by one, including Purandar, Shivaji knew he had to heed the subtle messages of negotiations that Jai Singh was sending out, simultaneously. It was now June of 1665.

The two men met; this time, on Jai Singh's terms. Shivaji came unarmed and agreed to most of the terms of the peace treaty. Among other things, Shivaji gave up as many as 23 forts, leaving him with only twelve, including his cherished one of Raigad.

In May 1666, Shivaji, accompanied by his son Sambhaji and a trusted soldier corps of around 250 men, left for Agra, amid much pomp and pageantry.

In Agra, things went badly from the very beginning. Shivaji was presented to the Mughal emperor, whose poor behaviour Shivaji proudly defied. Jai Singh and his son, Ram Singh – the latter was in Agra then – had promised Shivaji safety, but despite a ring of Rajput soldiers, it looked like Shivaji was unofficially under arrest.

Shivaji looked for every pretext to escape. In due course, an opportunity presented itself. It is said he and his son managed to sneak out while hidden in huge baskets of sweets offered as charity and gifts; another version says they left disguised as ascetics. In any case, Shivaji and his son made a difficult journey back to Raigad.

For the next three years, as he set about establishing orderly administration in the areas under his control (though unacknowledged by the Mughals), there was peace. But in 1669, Shivaji made attempts to reconquer the forts he had once possessed.

The attack on the fort in Sinhagad (Pune) was again carried out at night, as Maratha soldiers, led by their commander Tanaji Malusare, used rope ladders to scale the walls. Once inside, they resorted to hand-to-hand fighting. The fort was won, although Shivaji was deeply distressed at the loss of his trusted commander. Over the next few months, Shivaji won back his other forts: Purandar, Rohida, Lohgad and Mahuli; then, in 1670, Shivaji raided Surat a second time, once again obtaining much booty.

In the following years, Shivaji made continual incursions down south, seeking to claim the territories of his half-brother Ekoji. Following negotiations with the latter, he acquired the important Vellore Fort on the south coast.

His tactics and strategy had enabled Shivaji to carve out a kingdom for himself, one that would last under his successors, and whose legacy would be carried forward by able administrators-turned-rulers – the Peshwas –

for the next 100 years and more. In 1674, Shivaji, in an elaborate coronation ceremony was anointed king before other rulers, nobles and priests. He was accorded several titles, including that of Chhatrapati, which means 'supreme sovereign.'

Now, Shivaji set about rebuilding his kingdom and the region. He extended loans to develop and improve the land, encouraged resettlement in areas that had been abandoned, and also instructed his men not to disturb farmers during the agricultural season.

His administration relied on two main taxes: *chauth*, levied on lands not in Shivaji's direct control or those at the borders, was an amount paid in return for a promise by the Marathas to protect these areas; and *sardeshmukhi*, which was an amount over and above the land revenue, and it came to the king (Shivaji himself) directly. Besides these, he did not fundamentally alter existing rural structures. Shivaji also appointed *qazis* in places where Muslims were in a majority.

All through his days as conqueror, and then as monarch, Shivaji had dealings with the western trading companies. The latter had already set up bases in several port towns and cities of western India such as Surat (Gujarat), Rajapur (Maharashtra) and Goa.

The Portuguese, English and Dutch companies feared and admired him in equal measure. Shivaji often targeted their bases, as he did Surat in the early 1660s. But he well understood the benefits of trade and the other advantages the western traders brought with them. He negotiated

A ROYAL SECRET!

Shivaji carried out so many escapes that he had acquired an almost invincible status in the eyes of contemporary writers, travellers and witnesses. The British considered him equal to the conquerors of old, such as Alexander and Julius Caesar. As the writer Charles Kincaid wrote two centuries later, even eight months after the news of Shivaji's death, the British agents in Surat still advised caution, for such news had so often been wrong, that some had come to believe that Shivaji was immortal.

with the British for their much superior artillery. Moreover, noticing the efficiency of the Portuguese navy, he developed his own navy using the services of Portuguese and Goan sailors and mariners. From such early beginnings, the Maratha navy under Kanhoji Angre would become a feared force in the Arabian Sea, only a couple of decades after Shivaji.

Chhatrapati Shivaji Maharaj died in 1680, only a few years after his coronation ceremony. Sambhaji, his son, made the mistake of allying with Aurangzeb's rebellious son, Muhammad Akbar. In the ensuing campaign, while Akbar escaped to Persia, Sambhaji was caught, tortured and executed. Another branch of the family established itself around Thanjavur in the south. Sambhaji's son, Shahu, would become king in Pune, and it was from his time that the Peshwas rose to power, dominating Maratha politics for the next few decades.

WHAT AN IMPACT!

There was no ruler quite like Chhatrapati Shivaji Maharaj. He was adored by his followers, and feared by all his opponents. His campaigns and manner of conducting battle, and how he stood up to opponents, led to the rise of many a legend. Despite his short reign, the Maratha empire and state, especially under the Peshwas later, drew immense support from the peerless prestige of Shivaji.

TARABAI
Master Strategist

The daughter-in-law of Chhatrapati Shivaji Maharaj and the wife of his second son, Rajaram Bhonsle, Tarabai (1675–1761) came to the helm of Maratha affairs at a very crucial stage. In 1689, Rajaram was crowned Chhatrapati. He was only nineteen. Early on, he had to face the fury of Mughal forces, led by Aurangzeb himself, pressing into the Deccan, keen to recover the losses they had sustained when Shivaji had been powerful.

Sambhaji, Rajaram's older half-brother and Chhatrapati during 1680–89, was captured and executed by the Mughals, as Aurangzeb was angered by Sambhaji's support for his rebel son, Muhammad Akbar. The Mughals then launched attacks on Rajaram's strongholds in the Deccan, compelling him to seek shelter in the fort of Gingee in the south. He was helped in his escape by the forces of a

Rani Tarabai in battle

brave queen, Keladi Chennamma, who ruled over a small region in present-day central Karnataka.

Though Rajaram managed to evade Mughal forces, he died young, when he was only thirty, at Sinhagad Fort. In 1700, his wife, Tarabai, daughter of the brave general Hambirrao Mohite, who had died fighting the Mughals in 1687, assumed control of the Maratha empire on behalf of her son, Shivaji II, who was then only four.

Tarabai, then twenty-five, proved her mettle in her skilled use of cavalry and her adept military manoeuvring when she took on the Mughal forces. By 1700, the Mughal forces were tiring because the Deccan campaigns were long and arduous. The Maratha forces made several incursions across the river Narmada, reaching Malwa in the north Deccan. When Aurangzeb died in 1707, the Maratha forces were relieved, but this relief proved short-lived, especially for Tarabai.

The release of Sambhaji's son, Shahu, who had been in Mughal custody ever since his father's capture, led to a conflict for the throne. Both Tarabai – on her son, Shivaji II's behalf – and Shahu claimed the right to represent and lead the Marathas. Shahu was helped by his astute advisor, Balaji Vishwanath. Tarabai moved south to Kolhapur,

A ROYAL SECRET!

Tarabai was the daughter of the legendary Maratha general, Hansaji Mohite. Around 1673–74, as the Marathas under Prataprao Gujar, then general (or *sarnobat*) of the army battled the Mughals, in Nesari, now in Kolhapur, south Maharashtra, something unfortunate happened. Prataprao was killed and the Maratha forces would have scattered in chaos had Mohite not risen to the occasion. His effective command turned the tide of battle in the Marathas' favour. When Shivaji went to meet his forces at Chiplun, north of Nesari, he honoured Mohite with the epithet, 'Hambirrao' and made him general of the Maratha army. Hambirrao's sister, Soyarabai, was also one of Shivaji's wives; her son Rajaram would in turn, marry Tarabai.

where she set up base proclaiming her son as king of a rival Maratha kingdom.

Only two years later in 1709, another wife of Rajaram, Rajasabai, conspired to wrench Kolhapur for her son, Sambhaji II, and was successful. Tarabai and her son, Shivaji II, were placed in custody. When Shivaji II died in 1726, Tarabai reconciled with Shahu and went to live in

Satara. But Shahu had no heir of his own, and Tarabai's attempts at political manipulation were soon at play again. In the 1740s then, Tarabai made another attempt to re-establish the power she had lost.

As the story goes, she presented the infant Rajaram II as her grandson (Shivaji II's son) to Shahu, who then adopted him. Rajaram II succeeded Shahu as king but soon refused to do Tarabai's bidding. She had wanted him to oust Balaji Bajirao (grandson of the first Peshwa, Balaji Vishwanath) who had acquired considerable power as Peshwa. The drama unfolded quickly then. Rajaram II was imprisoned and proclaimed as an imposter. Tarabai, hoping to emerge as the truly powerful one, sought to instigate other nobles and officials to fight against the Peshwa.

Her efforts were finally unsuccessful. They only helped the Peshwa Balaji Bajirao – a general who was revered by his forces – to consolidate his own position. In the end, Tarabai surrendered in 1752. She died in 1761, a queen who loved to wield power.

WHAT AN IMPACT!

Tarabai sought to secure power for herself, claiming to represent the 'true heir' of Shivaji's dynasty. The power struggles between her and other claimants for Shivaji's legacy helped propel the Peshwas to power.

MANGAMMAL
Madurai's Munificent Queen

Nearly 120 years ago, travellers along the road that ran up north towards Madurai from present-day Kanyakumari in Tamil Nadu spoke eloquently of the banyan and cannonball trees that grew on either side. This road was once called the 'Mangammal *salai*', built by and named for a queen who ruled from 1689 to 1704. She belonged to the line of the strong Nayakkan rulers who dominated this region of Madurai (north, west and south Tamil Nadu today) since the decline of the Pandyas.

There were rumours that the road actually ran all the way to Benares, a holy pilgrimage town, and that the devout queen Mangammal had wells and places for rest built at regular intervals for the weary traveller.

Mangammal was in fact the queen regent of Madurai. She came to wield power in 1689 because her infant grandson, Vijaya Ranga Chokkanatha, was only three

A ROYAL SECRET!

In 1704, Mangammal was, as accounts suggest, thrown into prison and starved to death for she refused to give the throne up to her grandson. Still, it remains a fact that she was revered by her people for her charitable and generous rule, a time when Madurai recovered much of its old glory and honour.

months old when he was crowned king. But Mangammal's predominant role in Madurai's polity happened almost by accident. For one, she became her husband Chokkanatha Nayaka's chief queen only because his efforts for a marriage alliance with Thanjavur, a neighbouring kingdom, did not work out. After Chokkanatha's death in 1682, their son, Rangakrishna Muthu Virappa Nayaka became king, but he died in 1689. The heir to the throne was just about to be born when this tragedy struck.

Rangakrishna's wife, the disconsolate queen Mutammal, wanted to commit sati, but Mangammal dissuaded her. Yet Mutammal remained stubborn even after the birth of her son, the future king. As the story goes, she took poison and killed herself. Mangammal then had to rule as regent till her grandson Vijaya Ranga came of age.

Madurai was a rich trading kingdom, as it had been since Pandyan times. Mangammal found herself accosted to her west and north by enemies, while the Mughals under Aurangzeb were extending themselves far south beyond the Deccan. Mangammal reached a deal with Aurangzeb's general, Zulfikar Khan Nusrat Jang, who was fighting against Rajaram, Shivaji's son, at Gingee, north of Madurai. With help from Mughal forces, Mangammal took on Thanjavur. The rivalry between these two kingdoms had stretched for a generation or two.

She also compelled the ruler of Venad in the west, once a feudatory kingdom west of Madurai, to resume paying tribute. Mangammal's armies also waged war against Mysore (now Mysuru). In 1700, allying with Thanjavur, the two armies took on Chikka Deva Raya of Mysore. The latter had built an earthen dam, called an anicut, across the river Kaveri, whose waters were vital for the northern districts of the Madurai kingdom. As it happened, heavy rains struck just around the time the two armies met, washing away the anicut.

WHAT AN IMPACT

Mangammal was known for her political acumen, as well as her many public works. Her fine summer palace built around 1670 and called Tamukkam, is today a museum dedicated to Mahatma Gandhi. She made impressive donations to Madurai's famous Meenakshi Temple.

MARTHANDA VARMA

Rebuilding Travancore

Marthanda Varma (reign: 1729–58 CE), or 'the maker of modern Travancore', is known for being a far-sighted and reform-minded king. While he was ruler of Travancore, at first a small kingdom along the Malabar coast of Kerala, his forces waged and won a successful battle, fought on sea and land, against the powerful Dutch East India Company. This was in 1741.

The Dutch were then seeking a monopoly of the very profitable black pepper trade to the west, dominating smaller states and chiefdoms on the Malabar coast. The Dutch forces based in Ceylon (now Sri Lanka) took up the cause of one such small state, Kotarakara, and with their ships, moved west from Colachel (Kulachel), near Kanyakumari, towards Kottar. As they advanced further towards the Travancore capital of Kalkulam, Marthanda Varma, then in the north, quickly gathered his forces and marched south.

Marthanda Varma

The Dutch expected reinforcements from other Dutch colonies in Ceylon (Sri Lanka) and from Southeast Asia, but luck and time, and even the weather, were in favour of Marthanda Varma. His troops besieged the Dutch forces, and blocked their supplies. The rains also played spoilsport for the Dutch, when the gunpowder turned damp and didn't fire well. The battle fought between November 1740 and August 1741 ended in an overwhelming victory for Travancore. A victory pillar was erected in Kulachel by the government of post-independent India to mark this event.

Among the Dutch prisoners of war were the naval leader Eustachius De Lannoy and his deputy, Donadi. They both stayed on in Travancore and helped modernize its army. A string of forts along Travancore's northern border was strengthened and this helped during Travancore's later wars with Tipu Sultan of Mysore.

Following his victory over the Dutch East India Company, Marthanda Varma was quick to assert Travancore's position over smaller spice-producing and trading kingdoms of the coast. These included Kayamkulam, Ambalapuzha, Kottayam and Changanaserry, besides others. In 1753, the treaty of Mavilekkara (now in Kerala's Alappuzha district) signed with the Dutch stressed Travancore's royal

A ROYAL SECRET!

One of India's most celebrated painters, Raja Ravi Varma (1848–1906), belonged to the extended family of the Travancore royal house. Two of his granddaughters, children of his daughters, were later adopted into the royal family, for custom indicated that descendants would be recognized via the matrilineal line.

Ravi Varma's patron was the Travancore ruler, Ayilyam Thirunal (reign: 1860–80). The British administrator at Travancore, Edgar Thurston, helped Ravi Varma's works reach a wider audience. His paintings combined mythological themes with western influences, and were exhibited in Vienna and in Chicago in 1893 at the World Congress of Religions (where Swami Vivekananda made his much quoted address).

monopoly of the spice trade in the regions and sea routes it controlled.

Marthanda Varma reorganized internal administration too. The Nair aristocracy found itself edged out as Dutch officers were offered high ranks in the new reorganized army. Even the ancient trading community of Syrian Christians received encouragement. More significantly, a *dalavay*, similar to the prime minister of a modern state, was appointed to oversee the administration. One of Marthanda

Varma's most faithful and loyal officials was Ramayyan Dalavay, who served the kingdom from 1737 to 1756.

Marthanda Varma also established a relationship with the celebrated Padmanabhaswamy Temple at Thiruvananthapuram, reorganizing its revenue villages, performing the necessary ritualistic ceremonies and rebuilding it lavishly. He saw himself as the deity's 'vice-regent'.

His reforms and foresight helped his successors rule Travancore wisely. Dharma Raja, who came after him, successfully fended off Mysore's armies, and a later ruler, Swathi Thirunal, was a renowned music composer with over 400 compositions to his name. Travancore was justly known for its forthright queens who ruled in their own right or as regents – Gowri Lakshmi Bayi (1810–15), Gowri Parvathi Bayi (1815–29) and Sethu Lakshmi Bayi (1924–31). The last ruling king of Travancore, Sree Chithira Thirunal Balarama Varma, mandated the historic temple entry order in 1936 that opened up Travancore's temples to people of all castes. In 1949, it became part of Travancore–Kochi state and in 1956, the state of Kerala was created, absorbing all these older royal kingdoms.

WHAT AN IMPACT

Marthanda Varma understood the value of adapting the army to more modern needs at a time when kingdoms along the coast had to fend off powerful trading companies from the west.

TIPU

More than 'The Tiger of Mysore'

Born in 1750 CE in Devanahalli (in present-day Bengaluru district), Karnataka, Tipu Sultan was not just one of the chief opponents of the British East India Company, but was also highly feared by them. A fiercely independent ruler, Tipu (reign: 1782–99 CE) resisted British rule all his life, seeking alliances with neighbouring rulers in the hope of ensuring that Mysore (now Mysuru), the kingdom he ruled over, remained the important political and commercial centre he intended it to be.

The British, for their part, built up a fearsome image of Tipu Sultan to justify their conquest of Mysore by every means possible. The British called him the Tiger of Mysore, or 'Tippoo Sahib'. Public opinion in England considered him a vicious tyrant.

It was around 1761 when Hyder Ali, Tipu Sultan's father, appointed himself ruler of Mysore. The Mughal

Tipu Sultan

state was terribly weakened at this time. In the south, the successors of the Nizam of Hyderabad – a title adopted by a powerful Mughal noble who had declared himself independent when Aurangzeb's weak successors ruled in Delhi – constantly battled the Marathas and the Nawab of Arcot further south. Mysore, thus, had to pay tribute to whomever among these three could impose their will on it. Hyder Ali deposed the ruler of the Wodeyar dynasty of Mysore, and took the kingdom down a more militaristic, independent line.

From an early age, Tipu accompanied his father on military campaigns, assisting in both the First (1767–69) and Second Anglo-Mysore Wars (1780–84) against the British. During the Second Anglo-Mysore War, the British were defeated at the Battle of Pollilur. Later, Tipu, as sultan, had the battle scenes painted on the walls of his summer palace to celebrate his father's triumph. David Baird, a Scotsman in the British army, was taken prisoner during this war. He would, many years later, wreak revenge on Tipu by leading the final assault on Srirangapatna in May 1799.

The ancient island fortress of Srirangapatna, enclosed to the south and west by the river Kaveri, served as Tipu's capital. He was determined to build a rich and powerful state. So he tried to build up an alliance to drive the British out of India. His reaching out to the French, and to the Ottoman Turks, was also linked to his wish to develop Mysore industrially and improve trade relations with these countries.

Tipu's summer palace, Daria Daulat Bagh, is outside the fort at Srirangapatna. Hyder Ali began building the lavish palace in 1778. Tipu, who succeeded his father in 1782, completed the work two years later. The young sultan also constructed the Jumma Masjid, a domed mosque that towers above the town and has two lofty minarets, with a flight of about 200 steps leading to the very top.

By the early 1790s, Mysore was well off and well-organized, with viable trade routes, especially to the south, (where the spices and sandalwood forests were) and a European-style army. And its neighbours and other Indian princes, who had joined forces with the British against Tipu Sultan, feared the kingdom's ruler, with reason.

In 1785, Tipu's delegation departed from Pondicherry, a French territory, to France in search of a strong alliance against the British.

While the French, under Louis XVI, received the embassy cordially, their hands were tied. In the Seven Years War that ended in 1783, the British had soundly defeated France. This meant a loss of control in the high seas for the French. It also meant that they couldn't extend military help to territories in far-off Asia.

Louis XVI, whose life would end at the guillotine during the French Revolution of 1789, did send back artisans for watchmaking, china, glassware and, as the British spies reported (with considerable exaggeration), even rockets that could reach deep into the enemy camp. But in all, considering the proposed alliance, the mission was unsuccessful.

As a result, for several months after the delegation's return, relations between the French East India Company and Mysore remained chilled in southern India. Tipu extended Mysore's sway over the Kasargod Nayar dominions, rich in spice and sandalwood, that the French coveted.

This meant that when it came to fighting the British, Tipu was all on his own. The Nizam of Hyderabad and the Marathas were, in any case, already Mysore's sworn enemies.

The First and Second Anglo-Mysore Wars during Hyder Ali's time had been small battle engagements where the British had quickly retreated, accepting Mysore's superiority. But in the 1790s, the Third and Fourth Anglo-Mysore Wars would be more decisive, and it would be Tipu Sultan who would pay the price.

In 1790, Lord Cornwallis led the Company forces against Tipu. After three campaigns against Mysore – as part of the Third Anglo-Mysore War – Cornwallis managed to compel Tipu into submission. The Treaty of Madras was signed and Tipu was forced to give up half of his territory toward the south and east, and his sons as well, who were then aged eight and ten, as a guarantee for peace. His sons, though, were returned to him two years later.

The late 1790s were even more tumultuous. In 1798, with the rise of Napoleon and his world-conquering ambitions, the British could no longer play a waiting game in India and simply contain Tipu. The British now realized they needed to pre-empt Tipu from reaching out to France, and to Napoleon.

The Fourth, and final, Anglo-Mysore War took place in 1799. Lord Wellesley, the new governor general who had arrived in Calcutta (now Kolkata) in 1798, decided to settle the account with Tipu. An army of the British East India Company, including sepoys and horsemen, assembled in Madras under General Harris. The Nizam of Hyderabad sent a contingent, and Wellesley's younger brother Arthur Wellesley (who would later defeat Napoleon and be better known as the Duke of Wellington), led the British Thirty-Third Foot Regiment.

The invasion of Mysore began in February 1799. The Company army had taken its time travelling through dense forests, and rugged and rocky terrain. Elephants led the way, and there were thousands of bullock carts carrying equipment such as tents and supplies. There were also flocks of sheep and goats to provide meat for the officers. Many camp followers (servants and others, like cooks, grooms and washermen) and a travelling market went alongside.

The British army besieged the fort of Srirangapatna, despite the cannons staring down from its ramparts. Tipu then tried to reach an agreement with the Company,

A ROYAL SECRET!

The documents of objects seized from Tipu Sultan's treasury by the British have been recently discovered. These papers contain a detailed description of a popular exhibit in London's Victoria & Albert Museum – 'Tipu's Tiger' – which shows a Bengal tiger in the act of killing a British soldier lying on his back. The spoils also included Tipu's three hunting cheetahs. Tipu's throne was made of solid gold and extremely heavy. So it was destroyed, and the melted gold was distributed among the company's officers.

hoping to delay matters until the monsoon arrived, but the siege only lengthened.

Major General David Baird, who had been humiliated by Tipu's father in the Second Anglo-Mysore War of 1780–84, led the final assault. The long siege had exhausted Tipu's army and breaches in the walls were not repaired. This allowed the Company soldiers to rush in. Tipu rode out, dressed in his finest, laden with some of his most precious jewels, and fired away with his muskets.

But the odds were too great. The British versions tell us that Tipu was wounded and his soldiers tried to rush him to safety in a palanquin. But the party was stopped by an unknown enemy soldier and Tipu was killed for the fine jewellery he wore. It was much later, in the night hours, that the British soldiers found the sultan's body under a heap of corpses. He was given a honourable burial in his family mausoleum in Srirangapatna, just outside its fort. The doors of Tipu Sultan's mausoleum are inlaid with ivory, and there is a tiger-skin pattern throughout the tomb, echoing the sultan's fascination for tigers. Tipu's famed palace is now a museum, its murals of battle and court scenes displaying proud bygone times.

Mysore's abundant treasure was documented meticulously by British officials and then sent on to London. The British gave the kingdom back to a descendant of the older Wodeyar dynasty. Like in all dynasties and princely states in British India, he was a titular figure. The British made the decisions about most important functions such as defence and foreign policy.

WHAT AN IMPACT!

As a ruler, Tipu Sultan was ambitious and far-sighted. He knew the importance of setting up industries, and the threat the British posed. But his defeat in the last Anglo-Mysore War of 1799 showed that from then on there would really be no one to oppose the British East India Company. Soon after, the Company came to be in control of most of India, except the far north where Ranjit Singh still held sway.

RANJIT SINGH
Holding off Enemies

A formidable warrior, Ranjit Singh (reign: 1792–1801 and 1801–39) ruled an empire that extended from the river Sutlej in Punjab to the borders of Kabul and the Himalayan foothills. Like Tipu Sultan, he was feared by the British, who remained wary of taking him on in battle.

A big reason for this was the fact that Punjab occupied a strategic place. It was close to Afghanistan, beyond which lay Russia, always a threat to Britain's imperial might. In Mysore, Tipu Sultan had been easy to isolate, with the French always dithering on their promises to help. But Russia loomed very close like a 'Great Bear', and Afghanistan's amir always played a precarious, see-saw game.

Court writers describe Ranjit Singh, born in 1780, as being slight of build. An unfortunate attack of smallpox in his childhood left him blind in one eye.

Maharaja Ranjit Singh

Ranjit Singh's parents came from two different *misls* or chiefdoms/ small principalities of Punjab. His father, Mahan Singh Sukerchakia, was from the Sukerchakia *misl* and his mother, Raj Kaur, was the daughter of Raja Gajpat Singh of Jind. Their marriage united two *misls*.

The future ruler was only nine when he fought his first campaign against a rival chiefdom's city of Sardhana! His father, who was sick at the time, died before news of his son's victory reached him. Though Ranjit Singh was young, like Akbar, he too had the advantage of being mentored by two formidable women: his mother and then his wife Mehtab Kaur's mother Sada Kaur, who led the powerful *misl* of the Kanhaiyas after the untimely death of her own husband.

From 1795 onwards, Ranjit Singh had several brushes with Zaman Shah, the ruler of Afghanistan, for control over the cities of Peshawar and Lahore. Singh was skilled in the art of rapid manoeuvres – an immense gift when large armies had to be moved quickly and effectively.

Things took an unexpected turn during Zaman Shah's campaign three years later in 1798. In the midst of war preparations, Zaman Shah received news from Afghanistan that the Persians in the west were making rapid headway toward Kabul. In the rush to reach Kabul in time, Zaman lost 12 of his prized cannons in the river Jhelum, which was in spate. On receiving an urgent plea for help from the Afghani ruler to retrieve the prized guns, Singh generously complied. A grateful Zaman Shah assured Ranjit Singh that he would not oppose his taking over Lahore.

Ranjit Singh's first move on occupying Lahore in 1799 was to ride through the streets with his army, assuring citizens that they would be safe under the new dispensation. He was then only nineteen, and already master of one of the most historic cities of the subcontinent.

The maharaja's kingdom symbolized the political power the Sikhs had now acquired. Amritsar, the site of the Golden Temple, was considered sacrosanct, while Lahore, the most dominant city in the region, served as the political capital.

The administration of Lahore served as a model that Ranjit Singh replicated throughout his extensive territories. He did not want to be bound by constraints of political affiliations, family connections, regional and caste loyalties and suchlike. This was evident in the many capable outsiders, even foreigners, who willingly played a role in Ranjit Singh's administration or army.

After gaining Lahore, Ranjit Singh realized the need to bring all the *misls* under his control. The British and the Marathas, both powers who dominated regions south of Punjab, were a threat and a divided Punjab, broken into *misls*, could not stand up to them.

In 1804, he created an artillery corps, dividing them into heavy (bullock-drawn), light (horse-drawn), and camel-drawn artillery. In 1807, foundries that mass-produced copies of British guns were established in Lahore and Amritsar.

By 1808, his army comprised five battalions and his soldiers were armed with swords and a mix of European muskets and traditional matchlocks. By the time of his death in 1839, his army had nearly 30,000 men, including foreign mercenaries.

In the early 19th century Napoleon's threat became only too real. The French had conquered Egypt and there were rumours that they planned to advance into west Asia and beyond. In July 1807, Napoleon and Tsar Alexander I of Russia signed a treaty promising cooperation. Britain viewed this as a threat, especially as Persia had also been cajoled by the French to grant passage to the latter's armies. The British could not risk a war with Ranjit Singh now.

So the British put forward a treaty of 'perpetual friendship' with Punjab. The Sutlej Treaty was signed on 25 April 1809, with the river Sutlej as the boundary between Ranjit Singh's kingdom and the British Indian territories. The treaty recognized Ranjit Singh's right to certain territories he had already annexed south of the Sutlej.

With his southern border secured, Ranjit Singh turned toward strengthening and extending his kingdom in the north. A perfect opportunity arose when Zaman Shah's brother, Shah Shuja, now ruler of Afghanistan, fled to India after a challenging attack on his throne, taking with him the famous Kohinoor diamond. Shah Shuja, however, was captured by a rival warlord and sent to Ata Mohammed, governor of Kashmir. Shuja's wife, Wafa Begum, begged Ranjit Singh to rescue her husband and, in return, promised him the Kohinoor. Singh, however, bided his time.

In 1812, came the pretext Ranjit Singh had been waiting for. Wazir Fateh Khan, leader of the Barakzais (another tribe in Afghanistan), who wanted to get hold of Shuja (and through him the throne of Kabul), reached an agreement with Ranjit Singh to launch a joint invasion of Kashmir. Ranjit Singh and his army outsmarted the Afghans by reaching the strategic outpost of Shergarh (in present-day Pakistan) by a shorter and far more dangerous route. His forces also reached Shuja in time and rescued him, outwitting the Barakzais. And in doing so, Ranjit Singh secured Kashmir and the Kohinoor in one fell swoop.

Six years later, in 1818, when he acquired Multan Fort, the celebrated cannon known as Zam Zama also became part of Ranjit Singh's arsenal. Rated as one of the most formidable cannons in the world, it had helped Ahmad Shah Abdali win the Battle of Panipat against the Marathas in 1761. Interestingly, it is also mentioned in Rudyard Kipling's celebrated novel, *Kim*.

Multan was followed by Peshawar, a strategic frontier city, also in 1818. This city, a few miles from the Khyber Pass, was the gateway through which invaders from Central Asia had poured into India over the centuries. When a victorious Ranjit Singh rode into Peshawar after seizing it from the Afghans, he gave the same assurances to its citizens: that his armies would not indulge in carnage such

A ROYAL SECRET!

Ranjit Singh's youngest son, Duleep Singh, became king in 1843 when he was only five. His mother, Jind Kaur, was the regent, but three years later, the British resident took over the regency. She was exiled in Calcutta and Duleep Singh would see her again 13 years later. By this time, he had been 'moved' to London. Though it was a life of exile, Queen Victoria, the then British monarch, became fond of him. She was godmother to some of his children. He died in 1893 in Paris.

as burning holy books or desecrating places of worship. In 1820, Ranjit Singh led an expedition to Dera Ghazi Khan, a vital trade centre on the route to Central Asia, and to Dera Ismail Khan, another important city in the north.

From 1826 to 1838, Charles Masson, an American, roamed Punjab disguised as a beggar; he reported that under Ranjit Singh's rule, the state was better run and more prosperous than the parts of India under the British.

Around 1831, during Lord Bentinck's governor generalship, Ranjit Singh pressed for a written assurance of the continuation of the Sutlej Treaty and its promises of 'eternal friendship' between his kingdom and Britain. The British, however, kept their cards close to the chest. For at the same time, Bentinck had instructed Henry Pottinger, a British lieutenant, to prepare for a mission to Sindh to negotiate a treaty with the amirs that would open the river Indus to trade with Europe and the rest of India.

Ranjit Singh, citing the Sutlej Treaty, questioned the right of the British to negotiate with the amirs of Sindh. The British response was duplicitous. The deadlock on this matter remained through his lifetime.

On Ranjit Singh's death in 1839, a struggle for succession broke out, with court factions siding with one or the other of Singh's wives. After the British secured Sindh in 1843, the kingdom of Punjab that Ranjit Singh had built up so painstakingly was easy fodder for them, and in two Anglo-Sikh Wars (1845 and 1849), the British secured Punjab. The young king, Duleep Singh, was sent to Britain, and the immense treasure of the Sikh Empire, including the Kohinoor, went Britain's way.

WHAT AN IMPACT!

For at least three decades, Ranjit Singh ensured stability and security under his rule. He was a good administrator, a charismatic general and a master strategist. When he employed people from different regions and faiths in his service, he showed that a state or kingdom could best gain from the services of the most capable people.

AHILYABAI HOLKAR
A Life of Justice and Piety

In 1766, soon after the great Maratha general Malhar Rao Holkar died, his widowed daughter-in-law, Ahilyabai, petitioned Maratha Peshwa Balaji Baji Rao to recognize her right to rule Malwa, the dominion of the Holkar dynasty. Malhar Rao's son and Ahilyabai's husband, Khanderao Holkar, had already perished in battle a decade ago, killed while fighting on behalf of the Mughal emperor against the rebellion led by his wazir Safdar Jang. Ahilyabai had been only 28 years old then.

She had been married very young, at the age of eight, as was the custom those days. Malhar Rao Holkar had spotted her at a temple, carrying out duties, when he had stopped by at her village in Ahmednagar district (now in central Maharashtra). Impressed by her piety, he chose her as his daughter-in-law there and then, brought her to his kingdom, and married her to his son.

A stamp featuring Rani Ahilyabai

Ahilyabai moved to Indore, in north-west Madhya Pradesh, and in time, her father-in-law trusted her to run the big household and the local administration. By the time he died in 1766, Ahilyabai was an experienced leader. And since her son, Male Rao, was still a minor, she took on the regentship of Indore and Malwa. Her son, however, died within a few months from a mysterious illness.

However, James Malcolm, a British administrator who visited the region during Ahilyabai's reign, wrote how unpopular her son was. Male was notorious for troubling the pious and the poor. It appears that his death came as a relief for the people of Indore, the region's chief city, Maheshwar, where Ahilyabai lived, and for Malwa.

After her son's untimely death, Ahilyabai decided to become the ruler of Malwa. When there was opposition to her assumption of rulership, especially by a few chiefs, she marched out of Maheshwar, her capital on the south banks of the river Narmada, her bow quivers attached to every side of her elephant's howdah, to ask for the Maratha Peshwa's permission. Her determination and resolve impressed the Peshwa, who granted her the robe of investiture, making her the new ruler of Malwa.

For the next almost three decades, Ahilyabai (reign: 1767–95) ruled the region wisely and piously, as reported by

A ROYAL SECRET!

Ahilyabai's administrative skills were evident in how she reached a settlement with the Bhils and Gonds – migrant groups who lived in the forests and ravine areas around Malwa. They were known to harass traders, merchants and travellers. She decided they would keep a part of the toll but would safeguard the highways, and not harm those travelling on them. This was highly beneficial to Malwa, a kingdom through which trade caravans to the north and south passed.

James Malcolm. The region thrived under her benign rule. Located close to the heart of the subcontinent, the kingdom was important for trade, and a centre of cotton textiles.

Very early on, there had been a clear division of responsibilities. The army and the responsibility of fighting wars (in support of the Peshwa and the weakened Mughal emperor) went to Tukoji Rao Holkar, the adopted son of Malhar Rao Holkar. Ahilyabai was in charge of the kingdom's administration. As ruler, she was known for her just ways. She appointed as adviser someone who had actively opposed her, and this move effectively co-opted a possible rival to her rule.

She also made several charitable contributions to temples and dharamshalas, while she herself lived a simple

No. of Training	0
No. of Open Drawer	26
No. of logins	0

- All Khoya Sweet will last for three days from the date of purchase
- Khoya, Kaju , Badam items must not be kept in refrigerator
- Boondi Ladoo must be consumed within two days.
- GST extra as applicable.
- Kindly present the bill copy to collect food items from the counter.
- It is thermal paper generated bill. Keep xerox copy to retain.

Ptd. By : TPI

BIKANERVALA

TERMS & CONDITIONS:

- All Disputes are subject to Delhi Jurisdiction
- Goods once sold will not be taken back or exchanged
- All Bengali Sweet must be kept in refrigerator & consumed on the same day
- All Chaat items, Dokhla, Khandvi, Rabri, Rasmalai & Thali must be consumed within three hours of purchase
- All Khoya Sweet will last for three days from the date of purchase
- Khoya, Kaju , Badam items must not be kept in refrigerator
- Boondi Ladoo must be consumed within two days.
- GST extra as applicable.
- Kindly present the bill copy to collect food items from the counter.
- It is thermal paper generated bill. Keep xerox copy to retain.

Ptd. By : TPI

BIKANERVALA

life. Besides her prayers, she would spend the rest of the day in court, hearing pleas and complaints, settling matters of state, and dispensing justice.

Ahilyabai ruled till her death in 1795. Through her reign, peace prevailed in her small kingdom, while everywhere else there were tumultuous changes. For all the personal travails she went through – her daughter was widowed early and Ahilyabai had to talk her out of committing sati – James Malcolm writes that she was the beloved of her people. It mattered not that she had not ruled over a vast territory, nor increased the area under her control or even her wealth; it mattered that she had served her people, devotedly and selflessly.

WHAT AN IMPACT!

Indore and Maheshwar, which became her capital, thrived during Ahilyabai's time. She donated to many temples across India including those in Benaras, Rameswaram, Dwarka and Gangotri. Maheshwar is still known for its many temples and its saris. The handloom industry, as the story goes, was established by Ahilyabai who got in weavers from Gujarat and Malwa to weave the traditional nine-yard saris women wore for special occasions.

LAKSHMIBAI
Rebel and Martyr

After the British had subdued Mysore and Punjab, there were hardly any powerful rulers left in India. True, the Nizam of Hyderabad (today's Andhra Pradesh and Telangana) was a significant figure. But he only had a ceremonial army and no power to decide foreign policy. Moreover, the British now insisted that succession had to be vetted and approved by the authorities, usually the governor general and his council.

Lord Dalhousie, who came to India as governor general in 1840s, strictly implemented this policy, known as the Doctrine of Lapse (it was finally abandoned in 1859). As per this doctrine, if a kingdom had no proper male heir – someone who was a direct descendant of the ruling king – then the succession would 'lapse', and the kingdom would become a British province. Naturally, the princely states were furious, and the anger of these royal princes and rulers was one of the reasons for the First War of Independence in 1857 in several parts of north and east India.

Rani Lakshmibai

Another immediate reason for the uprising was the new cartridge seals introduced by the British. The Indian soldiers of several regiments of the British East India Company resented having to bite these seals since they believed it contained lard or pig fat – which was taboo for soldiers of both Hindu and Muslim communities.

In the kings who now faced the loss of their patrimony, i.e., the kingdoms they had expected to inherit, the soldiers found ready symbolic figures around whom to rally. Suddenly disinherited, rulers such as Nana Saheb, the adopted son of the Maratha Peshwa who was a king-like figure, also found in the soldiers a good support base to build up and challenge the British. And so, it was to Nana Saheb and his associate Tantia Tope that the aggrieved soldiers turned. But there was really no one quite as inspiring among the leaders of this war as Rani Lakshmibai of Jhansi.

Jhansi (now in present-day Uttar Pradesh) was a small kingdom. Lakshmibai (known as Manu when young) was the daughter of Morepant Tambe, who was in the Maratha Peshwa's service. She grew up in Bithoor, the Peshwa's base at the time, in the company of Nana Saheb and Tantia Tope, and was taught the skills of fencing, horse riding and even wrestling. At the age of fourteen, she was married to Gangadhar Rao, the king of Jhansi.

The following years saw tragedy befall the young queen's life. A son born in 1851 died in his infancy. Soon after, her husband's health took a turn for the worse, and it was when he knew his end was near that he adopted his nephew, Damodar Rao, as heir and successor. The adoption procedures were carried out in the presence of the British resident at Jhansi. However, after Gangadhar Rao's death, Lord Dalhousie, then British governor general, reneged on the commitment given by his own officials. He made moves to annex Jhansi as a Company territory. Rani Lakshmibai would have to leave Jhansi, and she would be paid a pension.

Lakshmibai (reign: 1853–54 and 1857–58) protested strongly, refusing to give up her Jhansi.

Things remained at a stalemate till the 1857 war broke out. As versions go, when reports of the soldiers' rebellion in Meerut reached Jhansi, Lakshmibai, at first, did not pick sides. In June 1857, a small battalion of Indian rebel soldiers entered the fort at Jhansi by assuring the British residents of their safety. This promise was, however, not kept and a large-scale massacre of British officers, some women and children as well, followed. Lakshmibai, caught amid this tumult, was faced with difficult choices. The British authorities asked her to maintain order till reinforcements came. But in August 1857, she was held responsible for the massacre, and a strong British contingent besieged the fort of Jhansi.

A ROYAL SECRET!

Among the more famous works on Rani Lakshmibai is the well-known poem in Hindi, *Jhansi ki Rani,* written by Subhadra Kumari Chauhan in 1927.

The siege lasted around four to five months. Then, in January 1858, taking advantage of some breaches in the fort walls, the British forces rushed in. It was then that Lakshmibai chose to escape. With her young son tied to her back, and armed with a sword, Lakshmibai jumped on her horse, leapt over the fort walls – as the story goes – and made her escape. Apparently, her trusted horse, Badal, died in the fall.

With a band of loyal guards, Lakshmibai and her son, Damodar, made their way to the town of Kalpi, to the north-east of Jhansi, and more than a day's journey away. In Kalpi, Lakshmibai joined hands with other rebel leaders such as Tantia Tope. But in May, when the British East India Company forces attacked, the rebels were soundly defeated. Once again, they broke up into groups and escaped.

Lakshmibai then took a course westward and moved toward Gwalior, whose fort was strong and had withstood several sieges. The rebels had already declared Nana Saheb the Peshwa at Gwalior. A huge British force with experienced commanders stormed Gwalior successfully.

There are different versions about how Rani Lakshmibai died. It seems she gave battle to the enemy, dressed in a soldier's uniform. Another version says she was badly injured, and as she did not want to be captured by the British, she asked someone to burn her body. In any case, the brave queen perished in the field of battle close to the majestic Gwalior Fort in June 1858.

She was cremated by the local people. The place where she is believed to have died is now a memorial. The fort at Jhansi, too, is a museum largely dedicated to her life. Barely a decade later, novelists and writers, British and Indian alike, extolled Rani Lakshmibai's heroism and strength of character.

It is not hard to figure out why Rani Lakshmibai remains so enduringly popular and beloved. She led from the front and her warrior skills were inspiring. The 1857 War of Independence had a violent and tragic end, but the rani's martyrdom underlined the reasons for which it was fought. In a time when most kingdoms were capitulating to the British East India Company meekly, Lakshmibai was determined in her resistance and died a hero.

WHAT AN IMPACT!

The rani's heroic resistance to the British symbolized the last battle of kings and queens against a powerful East India Company. From now on rulers would be mere titular figures. The War of Independence also ensured the end of the British East India Company's rule and India now became a colony under the British Crown.

SAYAJIRAO GAEKWAD
The Reformist King

As one of the leading Maratha families for over 150 years, and in the limelight since the Peshwas emerged on the Maratha political scene in the early 18th century, the Gaekwads had a distinguished legacy. They were based in Gujarat, with Baroda (Vadodara today) as their principal city. The British government – that had taken over the charge of ruling India from the British East India Company following the 1857 War of Independence – exercised tight control over them politically. But the Gaekwads were far more progressive and forward-thinking than many of their contemporaries.

It was during the long rule of Sayajirao Gaekwad (reign: 1875–1939) that some far-reaching reforms and developmental works were carried out in Baroda, making it one of the most progressive places in India, especially in the early 20th century. Working for the Baroda state became

Sayajirao Gaekwad

such a privilege that many people – administrators, scholars, engineers, musicians and other artistes – flocked to Baroda, seeking service there.

Sayajirao Gaekwad was not meant to be king. When Khanderao Gaekwad, the ruler of Baroda, died with no heir, his widow called an assembly of the extended family, especially those with young sons. Gopalrao (as Sayajirao was then known) walked with his father and brothers – he was the middle one of three brothers – all the way from Kavlana village in Nashik (Maharashtra) to Baroda – around 600 kilometres! He soon impressed the queen with his demeanour and his ready answers.

The British government vetted the queen's choice, and Gopalrao was anointed heir in 1875. He was also given a more royal-sounding name: Sayajirao. Since he was still a minor, the government also appointed a diwan, the very capable T. Madhava Rao, who had distinguished himself as an administrator in Travancore and Indore. The new king also had an English tutor, F.A.H. Eliot, who introduced him to a wide range of subjects and thinkers.

Sayajirao knew he had big shoes to fill. His predecessor, Khanderao Gaekwad, had initiated several projects, including the first narrow-gauge train to ply in Baroda state. Sayajirao, however, had help from his two main advisers: Madhava Rao and Eliot. The young king soon set about instituting some land reforms. He curbed the power of the '*sirdars*' who owned large amounts of land and coveted even more. Rao had some of their illegal gains converted into state land, and with fines and penalties, he had the *sirdars* cut down to size.

When Sayajirao came of age in 1881, certain disagreements with Madhava Rao led to the latter retiring to his family home in Mylapore (Tamil Nadu). But Sayajirao did not interfere with the reforms his former diwan had already instituted. Rather, he set about implementing his own.

The first matter that caught his eye was the education of girls. He established a girls' school that drew in pupils from the wealthy classes and the upper castes, and saw a daily attendance of around 50 students per day. In 1906, he became the first ruler to ensure free and compulsory primary education for everyone in his state.

His measures for health included the opening of a dispensary scheme all over Baroda state, offering smallpox vaccination to residents, and cleaning up the city so that the outbreak of cholera, which had claimed several lives in 1875, would not recur. The construction of the Sursagar tank, which would supply ready water to the citizens of the state, was also completed. Sayajirao improved the narrow-gauge train system set up by his predecessor. He also worked towards improving road transportation facilities, helped by Dinshaw Talyarkhan, an able engineer–administrator.

A ROYAL SECRET!

There is a story that has Sayajirao witnessing the flight of an unmanned aircraft developed by S.B. Talpade in 1895. This vehicle apparently contained liquid mercury that, by Talpade's calculation, would react with sunlight to produce hydrogen. Being lighter, this gas would enable the bamboo-constructed aircraft to fly. However, there are no reports confirming the maharaja's presence at an event that took place much before the Wright Brothers flew their first manned aircraft in 1903 in Kitty Hawk, in the state of North Carolina, USA!

It was under his supervision that Baroda inaugurated a central library. The university that carries his name even today – Vadodara's Maharaja Sayajirao (M.S.) University – was established in his time as Baroda College, and remained one of the most sought-after institutes for an education in the fine arts.

Capable men from all around flocked to the service of Baroda state, keen to serve as its administrators. Among them were future political leaders such as Dadabhai Naoroji, Aurobindo Ghose, Bhimrao Ambedkar, and the administrator–scholar Romesh Chunder Dutt. Among the key pieces of legislation the Baroda administration worked on were those ending child marriage and encouraging the remarriage of widows. The maharaja loved music too and the Baroda school held classical musicians such as Inayat Khan and Faiyaz Khan Saheb, both fine vocalists, in its fold.

Sayajirao died in 1939. He is remembered as a king who did not have to fight wars, but left a great impression for the reforms he instituted and the progress he brought to his state.

WHAT AN IMPACT!

Sayajirao encouraged brilliant and meritorious people to join his service, and supported them in the reforms they carried out in urban development, education and agriculture. The M.S. University in Vadodara, one of India's foremost academic institutions, began in 1881, when Sayajirao was the ruler, as the Baroda College. The Academy of Indian Music, founded by Ustad Moula Bux, was set up in 1886, for Sayajirao was a great patron of music. It is known for its majestic dome, inspired by the Gol Gumbaz of Bijapur.

A QUARTET OF BEGUMS

Far-Sighted Nawabs of Bhopal

When the Mughal Empire grew weak under Aurangzeb's successors, several smaller kingdoms emerged. Some declared independence outright; others chose to accept the overall authority of a more powerful ruler – by paying the usual tribute, while ruling more or less independently. The state of Bhopal, which emerged in the 1720s, was founded by Dost Mohammad Khan, a Pashtun from an area in present-day Afghanistan.

The state of Bhopal in central India included present-day Bhopal district and the areas around, including Raisen and Sehore. In the beginning, Bhopal had to fend off powers like the Marathas and the Nizam of Hyderabad, so it made sense for Bhopal's rulers in the early 19th century to seek an alliance with the British.

A treaty was signed between Bhopal and the British East India Company in 1818. This gave Bhopal's rulers – the nawabs

– much freedom in internal matters. For over a century, from 1819 to 1926, Bhopal was ruled by a succession of Begums, whose courage and far-sightedness enabled Bhopal to emerge as a centre of culture, learning, tolerance and prosperity. Even before, in its early days, Bhopal's queens – the wives of ruling sultans – had distinguished themselves in battle and as capable administrators. Dost Mohammad's wife Fatah Bibi had warded off the Rajputs and Marathas. And Mamola Bai, wife of a later nawab, was known to be a good administrator.

Qudsia Begum

In 1819, Qudsia Begum was not even nineteen when she became regent on the sudden death of her husband, Nazir Mohammad Khan. He was actually the son-in-law of the ruling nawab, Ghous Mohammad, who led a quiet life, and so the former had been ruling Bhopal as regent.

At a ceremony held soon after the young regent's death, it was his wife, Qudsia, who addressed the nobles, officials and the mourning public. Bhopal, she said, would continue to be ruled by the nawabs, and so the succession would pass on to their daughter, Sikander Begum, then only 15 months old.

What Qudsia had done was radical in several ways. She had addressed a crowd of people and chosen to do so unveiled, which went against tradition and conservatism. By insisting that her daughter was now nawab, Qudsia also emphasized that succession would remain within this particular branch of the family. It was expected that

Sikander would marry and it was her husband who would become the effective nawab, as had been expected of Sikander's own father (Qudsia's husband).

Following this, Qudsia took care to make her position more secure. While she had power in her own right, she was careful not to antagonize rivals. She also had Islamic religious authorities officially acknowledge her position and the fact that women could hold political positions and wield power in their own right. Qudsia was an expert rider and shooter, and regularly inspected the troops – a ceremonial but deeply assertive gesture.

Despite the fact that, in 1826, another son of Ghous Mohammad became the nawab, Qudsia Begum had the satisfaction of seeing her daughter, Sikander Begum, and granddaughter, Shahjahan Begum, rule Bhopal wisely and well for nearly 58 years between them (1844–1901).

Sikander Begum

Sikander Begum's tenure as regent began in 1844, on the death of her husband, Jahangir Mohammad Khan. Her daughter, Shahjahan, was then six, and as she was too young, it was Sikander Begum who ruled in her stead from 1844 to 1860. During 1860–68, she ruled as Nawab in her own right, as the British trusted her as a valuable ally in the years following the First War of Independence in 1857.

Sikander's mother, the formidable Qudsia Begum, had raised her like a warrior. Sikander had received military training, and like her mother, had never observed the customary purdah. Though her pro-British stance during the War of Independence made her unpopular with some officials and soldiers, Sikander Begum handled the matter practically. She raised the soldiers' salaries, and sent advisers, including her son-in-law, to negotiate with the miffed officials. She reformed the administration, reorganizing the state of Bhopal into more manageable districts, and also set up middle-level schools in Hindi and Urdu in every district. The Victoria School that she set up in Bhopal imparted technical training to girls in crafts like embroidery and woodcarving, while offering instruction in subjects such as Urdu and accounting.

In 1863, she made a journey to Mecca – the Haj – as all devout Muslims did. The travel account she wrote in Urdu was later translated into English in 1870. It remains an early example of a travelogue by a woman. When Sikander Begum died in 1868, her daughter Shahjahan became the ruler.

Shahjahan Begum

Shahjahan, who ruled from 1868 to 1901, was a practical and progressive ruler. One of her first acts was to ensure British support for her daughter, the ten-year-old Sultan Jahan, as her successor.

Shahjahan, unlike her mother and grandmother who were arch shooters and riders, was more culturally

A ROYAL SECRET!

The kingdoms of Bhopal and Pataudi, in Haryana, came to be related via marriage. Hamidullah's daughter, Begum Sajida Sultan (titular nawab after her father's death) was married to Iftikhar Ali Khan Pataudi, who played cricket for both England and India (post-Independence). His son, Mansoor Ali Khan Pataudi followed in his father's footsteps to become India's cricket captain in the early 1970s. His son is the Bollywood actor, Saif Ali Khan.

inclined. She had initially wanted to be a poet. As ruler, she did all she could to encourage the arts and culture in Bhopal. She wrote her own memoirs in Urdu, and encouraged poets, especially women poets, who lived in Bhopal. A reform manual Shahjahan Begum wrote in Urdu called *Tahzib un-Niswan wa Tarbiyat ul-Insan* or *The Reform of Women and the Cultivation of Humanity* had writings on women's work, their customs and traditions, and their lives as defined by the practice of Islam.

She made substantial contributions to the Mohammedan Anglo-Oriental College in Aligarh founded by Sir Syed Ahmed Khan in 1875. In her time, the first postage stamps were introduced in Bhopal and construction began for a railway line that connected Bhopal to Hoshangabad.

Sultan Jahan Begum

Sultan Jahan was 43 when she became Nawab on her mother's death in 1901. She and her mother did not get along. However, Sultan Jahan continued the efficient administrative practices of her mother. She helped found several educational institutions, just as her mother had done. She was also the first woman chancellor of the prestigious Aligarh Muslim University (formerly the Mohammedan Anglo-Oriental College). She also presided over the All-India Muslim Ladies' Association.

Begum Sultan emphasized health initiatives, ensuring awareness programmes for improved hygiene. In her reform of the bureaucracy, she highlighted merit and capability. In 1926, she abdicated in favour of her son, Hamidullah, who remained Bhopal's notional ruler till 1949. In 1956, Bhopal became part of the state of Madhya Pradesh.

WHAT AN IMPACT!

Both Shahjahan Begum and Sultan Begum built impressive buildings in walled 'mini cities'—Shahjahanabad and Ahmedabad (named after Sultan Jahan's husband)—within Bhopal. In the years 1899–1900, a severe famine, compounded by a failure of the rains, struck parts of India. But public works and welfare measures by both Shahjahan and Sultan Jahan, alleviated the people's sufferings.

DIGVIJAYSINHJI RANJITSINHJI
A Rescue in Time

Today, Jamnagar is a small district in the south-west corner of Gujarat. Till a few decades ago, that is, at the time of India's independence in 1947, it was a small princely state known, like Baroda, to have reform-minded kings. Its 19th century kings took a keen interest in civic planning, and much of present-day Jamnagar still has old whitewashed buildings – sometimes beautifully painted – neat, planned roads, and parks dotting the city.

The small state's 20th-century kings continued this tradition. By this time, the presence of kings and queens had become more symbolic. Even so, there were some rulers who did a world of good with their power to represent their state. One such personality was Digvijaysinhji Ranjitsinhji (reign: 1933–1948) – or as he was called, the Jamsahib – the king of Jamnagar.

Digvijaysinhji was, perhaps, already somewhat famous for being the nephew of the great cricketer Ranjitsinhji, who had distinguished himself as a fine cricket player while in England. Although Digvijaysinhji also played for the state and Bombay presidency in his youth, he never really had as distinguished a career as his uncle. In 1919, he joined the British Indian Army and served in Egypt in the early 1920s, and in Waziristan on the Pakistan–Afghanistan border soon after. He also served on several sports and government bodies, such as the Chamber of Princes and the Board of Control for Cricket in India (BCCI).

However, his finest hour came in the darkest days of the Second World War. Poland, in East Europe, was a bone of contention between Hitler's Nazi Germany and Stalin's Russia (then the Union of Soviet Socialist Republics or USSR). When the Soviet troops invaded east Poland, Germany still occupied the other half. This brutal invasion inflicted suffering on thousands of Polish people. While Jews were subjected to unimaginable horrors, ordinary Poles – women and children – were left homeless. Thousands more were 'deported' to faraway places in the Soviet Union.

As war raged, the USSR fell out of its pact with Germany in 1941 and reached a new secret understanding with the British, which included an agreement relating to the many Polish citizens still in Poland, who urgently needed help and rescue. An army unit called the Anders' Army helped

A ROYAL SECRET!

A documentary on Digvijaysinhji, *A Little Poland in India*, was made in 2015 by India's Aakar Films and the government of Poland. One of the Polish children who spent several months in Jamnagar wrote a book about it 50 years later: Maria van der Linden's *An Unforgettable Journey* was published in 1994. Anna Bonshek wrote about her father's life in Jamnagar in her book published in 2009: *Heniek: A Polish Boy's Coming of Age in India during World War II.*

transport hundreds of Polish women and children to Iran, via the Caspian Sea. Many found shelter in Iran, but in 1942, several hundred other Polish women and children were sent from Iranian ports, as well as from Palestine, on ships toward East Africa and India, where it was hoped they would find refuge.

Digvijaysinhji came to know of the plight of around 600 such women and children when their ship docked at Bombay (Mumbai) and its British governor refused any help. It was then that the Jamsahib stepped in, insisting that the women and children could live for a while in Jamnagar and consider it their new home. The Jamsahib followed up on his words with some resolute action.

Despite British disapproval, he ensured that the Polish women and children reached Jamnagar. He also had accommodation and a camp constructed at Balachadi, a village not very far from the royal palace. The war-torn and travel-weary refugees lived here and were looked after for four years, till 1946, when they moved to Valivade, another camp in Kolhapur in Maharashtra.

Some of the Polish refugees finished their schooling and stayed on in India, while some moved back to Poland when the Second World War ended in 1945. Many, however, did not wish to return to their home country as they had nothing and no one to return to. Some chose to settle in Britain, or elsewhere in other British colonies, such as New Zealand or Canada.

Even today, the Jamsahib is remembered at periodic meetings of the Association of Poles in India and a school bearing his name exists in Warsaw, the capital of Poland.

WHAT AN IMPACT!

Despite being the ruler of a small state, Digvijaysinhji did a world of good when he came to the aid of several hundred Polish women and children during the Second World War. In 2016, Digvijaysinhji was honoured in a special resolution by Poland's parliament, and he is sometimes affectionately referred to as the 'Polish Maharaja'.

DYNASTIES
A Short Chronology

It's not easy or possible to list all the dynasties that ruled in India and all their rulers in a small book. Here we have tried to introduce you to the main ones and it's important to remember that dynasties did not limit themselves to their areas of origin. This chronology lists dynasties from where they first grew in power and where they were largely dominant.

When we refer to 'India' in earlier times, it embraces the South Asian subcontinent: areas that now include Afghanistan, Pakistan, Bangladesh, Nepal, Bhutan and even parts of Myanmar, over which the Ahom kings of Assam and the rulers of Manipur in the east once held sway.

Then, of course, dynasties rose and declined over time. Some, such as the Guptas (mid-to-late 3rd century CE to around 550 CE), were powerful in ancient India. Others, like the Cholas, and the Pandyas in the south, held power for over a thousand years. They weren't consistently dominant; in some years they dwindled to a 'dependent' power and under a strong ruler they emerged as a force once again. In the text that follows, the dynasty's major years in power and its main rulers are cited. For the ancient kings, exact dates are hard to establish.

Ancient India: till 650 CE

◇ EAST INDIA ◇

MAGADHA

HARYANKAS

The Haryanka dynasty ruled Magadha from the mid-6th century BCE to around 415 BCE. It had powerful rulers like Bimbisara (r.* 543–493 BCE), and his son, Ajatashatru (r. 493–462 BCE), who first set Magadha on the path to greatness, taking advantage of its location and resources. Udayin, Ajatashatru's son, moved the capital from Rajagriha to Pataliputra. It remained so for later dynasties too. However, the later kings of this dynasty became tyrants, taxing the peasants heavily and doing little for their welfare. Nagadasaka (r. 435–413 BCE) was the last king of Haryanka dynasty. He was overthrown by his people, and Shishunaga, a Magadhan official, came to the throne.

SHISHUNAGAS

This dynasty began with Shishunaga (r. 413–395 BCE). He was an *'amatya'*, a high state official at Varanasi, when

* r. = reign

Nagadasaka was king. But a people's revolt made him king. As Magadha's ruler, he defeated the Pradyotas at Avanti. The later kings of this dynasty included Kalashoka. Apparently, like the Nandas, who came later, he was followed by nine sons in succession, with Mahanandin ruling last for almost two decades (r. 395–373 BCE).

NANDAS

The Nandas ruled during 345–322 BCE. Mahapadma, and his nine sons, including the last, Dhana Nanda, were in power for a mere 23 years or so. Dhana Nanda was defeated by Chandragupta Maurya. Today, the Nandas have come to epitomize despots. The Nandas were famous for their rich treasury and their army with a huge corps of elephants. As the story goes, Dhana Nanda is particularly remembered for insulting the political strategist and adviser, Chanakya (or Kautilya). It was this that later drove the latter to seek revenge.

MAURYAS

The Mauryas followed the Nandas. The three main rulers included its founder, Chandragupta I (r. 321 BCE–297 BCE), Bindusara (r. 297–272 BCE) and Ashoka (r. 268–232 BCE). The dynasty lasted nearly 200 years. The last Mauryan king, Brihadratha, ruled briefly (r. 187–185 / 180 BCE).

The Mauryas set up ancient India's first big empire, which extended from the north-west (in present-day Afghanistan) to the south near Mysuru in Karnataka. They were powerful conquerors, but both Chandragupta and his grandson, Ashoka, gave up war in different ways. Buddhism and Jainism had many adherents at this time. Chandragupta's adviser, Chanakya, wrote the *Arthashastra,* which detailed a king's duties and best practices for a state to function effectively.

SUNGAS

The last Mauryan king, Brihadratha, was killed by his commander Pushyamitra Sunga (r. 185–151 / 149 BCE) during an army parade. Agnimitra (r. 151–141 BCE), the second Sunga king, was known for his battle with Vidarbha, after he intervened on behalf of a cousin who staked his claim to the Vidarbha throne. The war led to Vidarbha being divided between the two claimants and both in turn accepted Magadha's suzerainty.

GUPTAS

Magadha's glory revived again under the Guptas (mainly 320–550 CE) who spread out from their centre at Pataliputra to rule over a vast empire that stretched to the north and west. The southern states and some hill states came under Samudragupta (r. c. 330–375 CE). Chandragupta II (r. 375 / 380–415 CE) was the greatest ruler of the dynasty, ushering in a 'golden age', but the period also saw a major battle against the Sakas (the Western Kshatrapas branch), whom he destroyed. During the reigns of the later Guptas, Budhagupta and Narasimhagupta, the Hunas made a series of incursions from the west. These raids depleted the revenues and weakened the dynasty, leading to its downfall.

KALINGA

The Mahameghavana dynasty ruled Kalinga for nearly 600 years, i.e., during 250s CE–4th/5th century CE. Its star ruler was Kharavela, who lived either in the 2nd or 1st century BCE. His Hathigumpha inscription describes him as one of Kalinga's greatest kings. Aside from being a great warrior, he worked for his people's welfare, building canals and reservoirs to help farmers during the dry season.

◇ CENTRAL INDIA ◇

AVANTI

Avanti is now in north-western Madhya Pradesh. Pradyota founded the dynasty here that took his name. He was a contemporary of Bimbisara and Ajatashatru. The beginning of his rule is uncertain, but he died around 520 BCE or so. He followed the usual policies of waging war and forging alliances. He fought with the king of Taxila, and ended his enmity with the king of Kosambi (near Prayagraj) with a matrimonial alliance. These would remain time-tested tactics for most kings.

◇ NORTH INDIA ◇

KANNAUJ AND THANESAR

The Pushyabhutis emerged in the late 6th century CE under Prabhakaravardhana, who ruled over an area around Thanesar (now parts of Haryana and Punjab). The most important ruler was Harshavardhana (r. 606–647 CE). Harsha, who was the younger son of Prabhakarvardhana, came to the throne in tragic circumstances. In battles with rival kings of Gaur (Bengal) and Malwa, he lost his older brother, Rajyavardhana, ruler of Thanesar, and his brother-in-law, Grihavarman, ruler of Kannauj (in the east), who was married to his sister, Rajyasri. Thus, to secure his kingdom that now included Thanesar and Kannauj, Harsha had to wage war on several fronts.

The Chinese pilgrim Xuanzang, who visited various kingdoms around this time, wrote of Harsha's magnificence and piety. The king was very charitable and a brave warrior. He lost to Pulakesin II and the river Narmada came to constitute an effective barrier between north and south India.

◇ NORTH-WEST INDIA ◇

INDO-GREEKS

The Indo-Greeks (180 BCE–10 CE) were an ethnic group that ruled in Afghanistan and parts of present-day Pakistan and north-west India. Menander (r. 165/155–130 BCE) was a follower of Buddhism. He is the king mentioned in the book *Milinda-Panha*, which records the many questions he asked the Buddhist monk, Nagasena.

INDO-SCYTHIANS

These formed another ethnic group that came from the north-west. They would later branch out into groups such as the Sakas and the Western Kshatrapas. Rajuvula ruled near Mathura around 10–25 CE. He defeated the Indo-Greek rulers of eastern Punjab and replaced their coins with his own. The Mathura lion capital, now in the British Museum, is dated to his reign. The Indo-Greeks made the gift of a stupa in Mathura to the Buddhists, according to old texts.

KUSHANS

These were one of five branches of the Yueh-Chi confederation, an Iranian or Tocharian Indo-European nomadic people who migrated from Gansu and settled in ancient Bactria. The Kushans (30–230 CE) asserted themselves from their centre in Peshawar, and their rule extended like a broad ribbon over the northern parts of present-day Afghanistan, Pakistan, and north India up to Mathura. They controlled parts of the Silk Route and the trade here made them wealthy. Under them, schools of sculpture at Gandhara (now Kandahar) and Mathura flourished. Their statues of the Buddha were marked by a delicacy of features and a close attention to detail. The important rulers were Kujula Kadphises (r. 30–80 CE) and Kanishka (r. 127–140/150 CE).

◇ WEST INDIA ◇

SATAVAHANAS

The Satavahanas, who dominated from the 1st century BCE to 2nd century CE, were once feudatories of the Mauryas. They waged a long war with the Saka satraps for the control of the western seaports, despite matrimonial alliances between them. Some early rulers such as Hala were great poets. Their inscriptions reveal the power of Satavahana queens and queen mothers. Some rulers derived their names from their mothers, such as Gautamiputra Satakarni, Vasishthiputra Pulumavi and Vasishthiputra Satakarni.

VAKATAKAS

The Vakatakas were allies of the Guptas. They were known for their patronage of the artistic activities that unfolded around this time in the Ajanta Caves. During the time of Prithvisena (r. c. 355–380 CE), the Vakatakas came close to the Guptas. Chandragupta's daughter Prabhavati, who married Rudrasena, Prithvisena's son, ruled as regent for her two sons after her husband's early death. Rudrasena II ruled for a mere five years (r. 380–385 CE).

Another Vakataka branch was based at Vatsagulma in eastern Maharashtra. Harishena (r. 475–500 CE) was involved in most of the rock-cut Ajanta caves. He was also a great conqueror and gained control over Avanti in the north, Kalinga and the Andhra kingdom in the east, and Lata in Gujarat.

WESTERN KSHATRAPAS

They were a sub-branch of the Sakas who held power in the west, in present-day Saurashtra and eastern Rajasthan, during 45–405 CE. The Kshatrapas were chieftains and later carved out an independent kingdom. Rudrasimha III (r. 380–395 CE) proved to be a great menace to the Guptas till he was defeated by Chandragupta II.

SOUTH INDIA

PANDYAS

Among the longest-lasting dynasties, their power waxed and waned for nearly 1,500 years till they were defeated by Alauddin Khilji's armies in the early 14th century. They are mentioned in Sangam literature (300 BCE–300 CE).

The Early Pandyas are believed to have thrived for these 600 years. Pandion (c. 50 BCE–50 CE) was one of the early kings. Nedunjcheliyan (late 3rd century BCE), is credited with staving off an invasion from the north. This victory was commemorated in a long poem called *Maduraikkanchi*. He was also the king mentioned in the epic *Silappatikaran*.

The Pandyan kingdom returned to prominence during 6th–10 centuries CE. Kadungon (r. 590–620 CE) revived the kingdom when the Kalabhras were defeated. First, they ruled from Korkai in the south, and then moved up north towards Madurai. His son and successor Avani Sulamani (r. 620–645 CE) was as great a ruler as his father.

Rajasimha Pandian (r. 905–920 CE) was famous for the battle of Thirupirambiyam, when he saw off the forces of the Pallavas, the Western Gangas and the Cholas.

The Pandyan Empire (13th–14th centuries), saw a 'golden age' under Jatavaram Sundara Pandya (1251–68 CE). He expanded the kingdom up north towards present-day Andhra Pradesh. They also conquered north Ceylon (Sri Lanka). Their fortunes again waned with the rise of the Cholas. But in the 13th century, the Pandyas rose again, troubling the Cholas, the Cheras and the Sinhalese. Vira Pandya (r. 1309–45 CE) faced off with the Khiljis of the Delhi Sultanate. The city of Madurai was besieged, but finally Malik Kafur, Alauddin Khilji's general, gave up.

CHERAS

The Cheras (1st–4th century CE) made up one of the three major dynasties of ancient Tamil Nadu, besides the Cholas and Pandyas. They traded in spices with west Asia and the Mediterranean countries. But not much is known of the actual area under their control. In the beginning, they ruled over areas in present-day Kerala and Tamil Nadu. The ancient city of Muziris on the Malabar coast was a flourishing

Chera centre. We know about them from the ancient text *Pathitruppaththu* by the poet Kannanar. Uthiyan Cheralathan was an almost mythical conqueror. He fought a great battle against Karikala Chola and, though injured, he still fought on bravely. The story goes that he starved himself to death, in the manner of ancient kings, and some of his devoted ministers followed him in the act.

Imayavaramban Nedum Cheralathan was another great Chera ruler praised in the book written by the poet Kannanar. He fought against the Kadambas, and captured foreign or *yavana* traders on the Malabar coast, who had been oppressing the local fishermen. In battles against the Chola ruler, both kings lost their lives.

Some centuries later, the Cheras came to be identified with the **Kulashekharas** (800–1120 CE). This dynasty's important rulers were Kulashekhara Varma (r. 800–20 CE), and Ramavarman Kulashekhara (r. 1089–90 or 1102–22 CE). The last king of the Cheras, Perumal, had an advisory council of four ministers more powerful than the king. Perumal also fought successfully against the weakened Cholas in the east.

CHOLAS

The Sangam Cholas (early 3rd–2nd century BCE to 4th century CE) had Karikala Chola (1st or 2nd century CE) as their most famous ruler.

The imperial Cholas remained in prominence between the 10th to the 13th centuries CE. There was a huge battle of succession after Parantaka II (r. 957–970 CE) when two sets of cousins claimed the throne. Finally, some stability was achieved in the reign of Rajaraja (r. 985–1014) and Rajendra (r. 1014–44 CE). The Cholas were master strategists. Their navy sailed across the Bay of Bengal to Southeast Asia and even up the Malabar coast in the west. The Chola queens were patrons of art and built temples.

In the time of Kulattonga Chola (r. 1070–1122 CE), diplomatic relations with China showed the wide influence the Chola empire had. By mid-13th century, they suffered attacks from their neighbours, including the rejuvenated Pandyas, the Hoysalas and smaller kingdoms to the west.

CHALUKYAS

The first branch of the Chalukyas, which flourished during 543–753 CE, was centred at Badami in present-day Karnataka. The **Badami Chalukyas** included rulers like Pulakesin I (r. 540–566 CE), Kritivarman I (r. 566–597 CE) and Mangalesha (597–609 CE), before Pulakesin II became king (r. 609–642 CE). A great ruler, he was known for his thirst for conquest.

His brother, Kubja Vishnuvardhana, who was first governor of Vengi in the east, established the **Eastern Chalukya** dynasty that emerged as a power in its own right.

Pulakesin's successors continued the conflict with the Pallavas, sometimes dashing far into Kanchipuram, taking away objects of beauty and craftspersons to beautify their own capital. The Pallavas retaliated in equal measure. Badami acquired a reputation as a centre for cultural excellence. Later rulers like Vikramaditya I (r. 655–680 CE), Vijayaditya (r. 696–733 CE) and Vikramaditya II (r. 733–746 CE) were brave warrior kings.

There were two branches of the Chalukyas that remained in force even after the dynasty at Badami had declined.

The **Eastern Chalukyas** thrived in the Vengi region (eastern Andhra Pradesh, around the rivers Krishna and Godavari) till 1189 CE, despite the fact that the Rashtrakutas now held power in this western part of south India (Karnataka) and western Deccan, following the decline of the Chalukyas at Badami.

A third branch of the Chalukyas emerged when Tailapa II (r. 957–997 CE) set up the **Western Chalukya** dynasty or the Chalukyas of Kalyani (their capital, in present-day Karnataka). The Rashtrakutas had been weakened following an invasion from the northern Paramara king, Siyaka II, in the mid-10th century. The last Rashtrakuta king, Karka II, was known to be brutal and many officials deserted their ranks. Tailapa took this opportunity to declare his independence. He waged battle against the Paramaras, the Latas of Gujarat, and Uttama Chola in the south. The Kalleshvara Temple in Davengere district of Karnataka is attributed to him.

7th–12th Century CE

◇ SOUTH INDIA ◇

PALLAVAS

The scions of this southern dynasty (275 CE–897 CE) are known for their freestanding temples at Mamallapuram and their long-running conflict with the Chalukyas. They traded with their ships across the Bay of Bengal and even controlled northern Ceylon (Sri Lanka) for a time.

The three rulers, Mahendravarman I (r. 600–630 CE), Narasimhavarman I (r. 630–668 CE) and Rajasimhan or Narasimhavarman II (r. 700–728 CE), who among them ruled for a glorious 130 years, waged wars against the Chalukyas and the Cholas, and built beautiful temples. In their time, Tamil got much encouragement.

◇ WEST INDIA ◇

KADAMBAS

The Kadambas (345–525 CE) ruled in north Karnataka and Konkan. They had their capital at Banavasi and were contemporaries of the Western Ganga dynasty. They encouraged Kannada as a literary language.

The first Kadamba king was Mayurasharma, whose reign began in 345 CE. He was humiliated by the Pallavas of Kanchi and took his revenge by defeating them. Later, they became feudatories of the Chalukyas and the Rashtrakutas. Around the 6th century CE, the Kadambas broke up into smaller branches ruling at Goa, Hangal and Halasi, and as feudatories of the older dynasties.

MAITRAKAS

This dynasty (475–767 CE) ruled from the capital Valabhi in Gujarat (Saurashtra), coming to power after the fall of the Guptas. They were generals, who later became independent. They came in the crossfire when Harsha and Pulakesin fought. They built a monastery at Valabhi besides several Buddhist and Jain temples, of which not many have survived.

KALACHURIS

Ruling from Kalyani (western Deccan) in east–central India, the Kalachuris (550–620 CE) were once the feudatories of the Guptas and the Vakatakas. They are believed to be behind the temples of Elephanta and Ellora. The coins of one of their kings, Krishnaraja, were found near the Shiva temple on Elephanta Island. They were later defeated by the Chalukyas of Badami and became their feudatories.

RASHTRAKUTAS

The early Rashtrakuta rulers like Dantidurga (r. 735–756 CE) and Krishna I (r. 756–774 CE) asserted their independence when the Chalukyas of Badami declined in power. They had their sights set on Kannauj. Rulers like Govinda II (r. 774–780 CE) and his successor, Dhruva (r. 780–793 CE) spent almost their entire lives on the march, as they crossed the river Narmada to fight the Pratiharas.

Amoghavarsha (r. 814–878 CE), who ruled for almost 64 years, was far wiser. He entered into matrimonial alliances with neighbours and employed Arabs as soldiers and officials. The Arab traveller, Sulaiman, spoke highly of him, calling him the wisest of all kings. The Rashtrakutas finally dominated for over two centuries (753–982 CE).

WESTERN GANGAS

The Western Gangas (350–1000 CE) ruled over an area comprising the northern ends of Kerala, Tamil Nadu and Karnataka. Durvinita (r. 529–579 CE) was one of their bravest rulers. He fought the Pallavas, who tried to oust him with the help of the Kadambas. He was also a great scholar and wrote a Sanskrit version of the *Brihatkatha*, originally written in a Prakrit dialect. The great Sanskrit scholar, Bharavi, lived at his court for a while and wrote the famous *Kiratarjuniyam*, a battle mentioned in the Mahabharata between Arjuna and Shiva, disguised as a hunter.

PARAMARAS

Among the rulers of the Paramara dynasty (9th/10th centuries–1305 CE), Bhoja (r. 1010–55 CE) was a polymath and no mean warrior. His kingdom centred in Malwa, and he was the founder of the city of Bhojpur in Raisen, central Madhya Pradesh. His struggle against his uncle, Munja, who also vied for the throne, inspired works composed 2-3 centuries later, like the *Prabandha Chintamani* and the *Bhoja Prabandha*. He established an academic centre, the Bhoja Shala, where Sanskrit was taught and literary works composed in it. The Bhojeshwar Temple in Bhojpur is one of the many temples attributed to him. He possibly formed an alliance with the Cholas in the south and the Kalachuris in the west. But there were endless wars with Bhima, the Chalukya ruler, and Karna of the Kalachuris in western Deccan.

NORTH INDIA

GURJARA PRATIHARAS

This dynasty (mid-8th century–1036 CE) dominated western India, i.e., areas of today's Rajasthan and Gujarat and north Madhya Pradesh. They were constantly battling the Rashtrakutas and the Palas for control of Kannauj. The first ruler, Nagabhata I (r. 730–756 CE), saw off incursions by the Arabs who had conquered Sindh. Mihira Bhoja (r. 836–886 CE) was a king who encouraged learning of all kinds.

CHAHAMANAS/CHAUHANS

The Chauhans (mid-8th to mid-12th centuries) ruled over Ajmer but took control of Delhi in the time of Visaldeva (mid-12th century). They had a long-running enmity with the Arabs of the north-west who kept invading this region. Visaldeva was known for his buildings and love of Sanskrit. His nephew Prithviraj III (r. 1165–92 CE) gained legendary status for his battles with Muhammad of Ghor in Tarain (1191 and 1192), and his rivalry with Jaichand of Kannauj. His stories have been immortalized in the *Prithviraj Raso*, composed several decades after his time.

CHANDELAS

This Chandelas of Jejakabhukti (9th–13th centuries CE) came after the Gurjara Pratiharas. They controlled a small region in present-day northern Madhya Pradesh. Hemmed in on all sides by kingdoms like the Palas, the Rashtrakutas and the Sultanate dynasties in Delhi, its rulers, like Yashovarman and Dhanga, had to constantly wage war on all fronts. They were known for the temples they built at Khajuraho.

SOUTH INDIA

YADAVAS/SEUNAS

The kingdom of the Yadavas/Seunas (850–1334 CE) of Devagiri at one time stretched from the river Narmada to the river Tungabhadra, and comprised parts of modern Maharashtra and Madhya Pradesh.

In the early 13th century, Simhana II (r. 1200/1210–1246 CE) defeated the Hoysalas and fought the Chalukyas for control of the Lata region in Gujarat. He defeated the Paramaras, the Kakatiyas and the Shilaharas. The writer and poet Sarangadeva lived in his court and wrote the *Sangita Ratnakara*.

Ramachandra (r. 1271–1311 CE) had to face defeat when Alauddin Khilji's armies invaded the Deccan.

HOYSALAS

Based in the southern Deccan, the Hoysala dynasty (1026–1343 CE) produced a large body of literature in Sanskrit and Kannada. Their original home was in the hill areas north-west of Dorasamudra (Karnataka) and they spread out towards the rich Raichur doab, between the river Krishna and its tributary, the river Tungabhadra.

At first, they were feudatories of the Chalukyas of Kalyani. Vishnuvardhana (r. 1108–52 CE) was their first great king, who defeated the Cholas to the southeast. His grandson Ballala II (r. c. 1173–c. 1220 CE) defeated the Yadavas. Vira Someshwara (r. 1235–1263 CE) secured control of the fertile Kaveri area. Their great rivals were the Cholas and the Pandyas. It was Ballala III (r. 1292–1343 CE) who supported the Delhi Sultanate against the Pandyas and it cost him dearly, for soon after the Khilji armies had defeated the Pandyas, they turned to Hoysala. In two decades, he was defeated by the Tughlaq armies that would exact heavy tributes from him.

They built unique zigzag temples, on a star-shaped platform, with walls packed with carvings, such as the

Chenakeshava Temple at Belur and the Hoysalesvara Temple at Halebidu in present-day Karnataka.

KAKATIYAS

The Kakatiyas (1163–1323 CE) traced their origin to a legendary chief, Durjaya. They were earlier vassals of the Rashtrakutas and then the Chalukyas. They ruled in the northern Telangana region before moving towards the eastern coast and southward. The fort of Warangal was believed to be the strongest fort in medieval India.

One of the longest ruling queens of Indian history, Rudrama (r. 1261–95 CE) later abdicated in favour of her grandson, Prataprudra II (r. 1289/1295–1323 CE), who had to constantly wage battle against the Delhi Sultanate – first the Khiljis and then the Tughlaqs. He had to pay tribute to Alauddin Khilji. He first won against Muhammad bin Tughlaq's forces, but, in 1323, he committed suicide on the banks of the Narmada while being taken as a prisoner to Delhi by the Tughlaqs.

EAST INDIA

PALAS

The Palas (8th–12th century CE) ruled over the region of Bengal. The first Pala king Gopala (r. 750–780s CE) was elected by his people. The Palas waged long battles against the Pratiharas and Rashtrakutas for the city of Kannauj. These battles were especially frequent when Dharmapala (r. 770s–810s CE) and Devapala (r. 810s–845 CE) were rulers. In the time of Mahipala I (r. 970s–1025 CE), the Chola armies under Rajendra Chola invaded the Pala kingdom. The Palas were patrons of learning and the universities of Nalanda and Vikramshila flourished in their time.

SENAS

The Senas (1070–1230 CE) claimed to be originally from Karnataka. Ballala Sena (r. 1159–79 CE) made Nabadwip in east Bengal his capital and married a princess of the Western Chalukya dynasty. Nabadwip is famous as the birthplace of the saint–poet Chaitanya.

Lakshmana Sena (r. 1179–1204 CE) was a great conqueror who expanded the Sena kingdom towards present-day Assam, Odisha and as far up north as Varanasi. In the time of Qutbuddin Aibak in Delhi, his general Bakhtiyar Khilji brought the western part of Bengal under Sultanate control. The Senas continued to hold eastern Bengal for a few more decades. Jayadeva, who wrote the *Gita Govinda*, was at the court of Lakshmana Sena.

EASTERN GANGAS

The Eastern Ganga dynasty (1078–1434 CE) ruled over most of present-day Odisha and parts of Chhattisgarh and

Andhra Pradesh. They were known for their trade links with Southeast Asia, and for building temples, such as the Konark Temple and Puri's Jagannath Temple. They had matrimonial links with the Chola empire and so the later rulers called themselves Chodagangas.

Anantavarman Chodaganga's (r. 1078–1147 CE) mother was a Chola princess. He conquered Utkala, Kalinga and Kosala. Later rulers had to fend off attacks from the Delhi Sultanate and the rulers of Bengal. Narasimhadeva I, in the 13th century, conquered Bengal, and built the Konark Temple to mark his victory. He also married princesses of the Chola and Paramara dynasties.

ASSAM

VARMANS

The Varman dynasty ruled in ancient Assam. Its most important ruler, a contemporary of Harsha, was Bhaskaravarman in the 7th century CE. Xuanzang visited his kingdom and for so long that Harsha was incensed. He threatened to send an army against Bhaskaravarman, who soon sent Xuanzang back!

AHOMS

Among the Ahoms (1228–1826 CE), as many as 43 kings ruled for over 600 years. The first king, Sukaphaa (r. 1228–68 CE), was said to be born in Yunnan in present-day south-west China. In line to succeed his uncle as king, he was forced to leave home after his aunt gave birth to a son. Crossing the river Irrawaddy in the north, he first defeated a Naga tribe and then entered the Brahmaputra valley in Namrup. He encouraged his followers to marry among local groups. Charaideo, the capital he founded, remains a symbolic centre even today.

Another king, Suhungmung (r. 1497–1539 CE), made his kingdom inclusive by reaching out to other ethnic groups. He defeated the Kacharis to the south and Kamatas to the west.

Sukhaamphaa, who ruled for over 50 years (r. 1552–1603 CE), was known for his love of sports. A severe injury while elephant hunting gave him a permanent limp and the nickname, 'khora' or 'khora-raja'. During his reign, the battles with the Koch kingdom in north Bengal continued. The British intervened in Assam in the 1830s during the Anglo-Burmese wars and annexed it soon after.

MANIPUR

MEITEIS

The Meitei kings ruled Manipur for nearly 1,500 years (1445 BCE–799 CE). Manipur was known as Kangleipak in ancient times. In the 13th century BCE, under the Meitei kings, the game of polo was apparently first played in Manipur.

NINGTHOUJAS

Soon after it was the Ningthouja dynasty that dominated Manipur for over 1,000 years (8th–18th centuries CE).

Pamheiba (r. 1709–1754 CE) was an important ruler. He was a warrior who constantly waged battles against his neighbours – Tripura to the east and Burma to the south. He was known to have accepted Hinduism and changed his name to Garibnawaz Pamheiba.

His grandson Ching-thang Khomba has acquired almost mythical status. It was in his reign that the famous Ras Lila dance became popular. There are stories that his uncle who had usurped the throne wanted to kill him and the god Vishnu saved Ching-thang time and again by whispering advice to him in dreams. As king, he became a devotee of Vishnu. During his time, the British East India Company made overtures to the kingdom, and renamed it Manipur from Meitrabak.

NORTH INDIA

KASHMIR

KARKOTAS

It was the Karkotas who ruled Kashmir around the 7th–8th centuries CE. Their best-known king was Lalitaditya Muktapida (r. c. 724–760 CE). He was a great conqueror and had Chinese help in conquering areas to the north-east, i.e., Ladakh. He also defeated Yashovarman of Kannauj in the 8th century CE. He built the Martand Sun Temple at Anantnag. Several Buddhist temples were built during this time.

UTPALAS

The Utpala dynasty followed (9th–12th centuries CE), of whom Anantivarman (r. 855–883 CE) is the best-known. His minister Suyya carried out many engineering works, such as desilting the river Jhelum. Several temples and monasteries too were built in his time, after which civil wars took over.

LOHARAS

In the time of the queen Didda (11th century CE), the regions of Lohara (possibly north-west Kashmir or Pir Panjal) and the Kashmir valley came together. Didda was a daughter of a Lohara king and married to the king of Kashmir. Didda's manipulations to stay in power caused instability for several years.

KASHMIR SULTANATE

The Kashmir Sultanate ruled this region during 1346–1580s CE. Zain-ul Abidin (r. 1420–1470 CE) suppressed the chiefs of Ladakh and Baltistan. He was known for his love of learning and himself knew many languages. The Mahabharata and Kalhana's *Rajatarangini* were translated into Persian in his time. He was called 'Budshah' or great king because of his tolerance for people of all faiths. He built canals and bridges, and gave responsibility to village communities.

13th Century Onwards
NORTH INDIA

Delhi Sultanate
MAMLUK/SLAVE DYNASTY

Qutbuddin Aibak first served Muhammad of Ghor as a *mamluk* or slave, and led Ghurid armies in battle. But soon after Muhammad's death, under Qutbuddin and Iltutmish, his successor and son-in-law, the Mamluk dynasty (1206–89 CE) showed an independent streak. The Qutub Minar was built by the first two slave kings in honour of a Sufi saint. Iltutmish made a radical decision to make his daughter Razia his successor. Under Razia, and Balban who came later, the challenge was to constantly balance different factions of the nobles.

KHILJIS

Alauddin Khilji's (r. 1296–1316 CE) love for gold led him into many battles. He was a complex man and a ruthless general, who made successful conquests in regions far down south such as Madurai of the Pandyas, and Halebidu, ruled by the Hoysalas. He was a capable administrator, thwarting Mongol attacks and ensuring a period of peace for Delhi and its neighbouring regions.

TUGHLAQS

Muhammad bin Tughlaq (r. 1325–51 CE) was a king with grand ideas, who made so many mistakes that his cousin and successor Firuz Shah (r. 1351–1388 CE) was unable to set them right. Between them, they ruled for 60 years, but couldn't save the empire. Muhammad bin Tughlaq's ill-conceived schemes left Firuz Shah with no resources for his welfare measures, the army was too huge to maintain, and the empire had grown well beyond its means.

SAYYIDS

The Sayyids (1415–1451 CE) were appointed governors by Amir Timur, who invaded Delhi and its surrounding areas in 1398 CE. They did not leave much of a mark. The tomb of the second Sayyid ruler, Muhammad Shah, stands in Delhi's Lodhi Gardens.

LODHIS/LODIS

The Lodhis (1451–1526 CE), who are regarded as the last of the Delhi sultans, remain known for their gardens and tombs around Delhi. Sikandar Lodhi was said to be the founder of Agra. He was an accomplished poet and encouraged translation of works of Sanskrit into Persian. But his successor Ibrahim Lodhi antagonized too many nobles, who invited Babur to invade India.

◇ WEST INDIA ◇

DECCAN

BAHMANIS

The Bahmani Sultanate (1347–1527 CE) came into being in the last years of the rule of Muhammad bin Tughlaq when Alauddin Bahman Shah revolted along with other nobles in 1347. Born Hasan Gangu, he not only gave himself a new name, but also a new capital city as he moved from Daulatabad to Gulbarga (Hasanabad). In 1425, he moved to a new capital called Muhammadabad in Bidar. The sultanate encouraged Persian literature and the adoption of Persian cultural standards in everyday life.

The kingdom always had twin concerns – to expand and block attempts at encroachment by other kingdoms around it, like Malwa and Gujarat to north, the Odisha and Reddi kingdoms, and the Vijayanagara kingdom to the south.

Firuz Shah (r. 1397–1422) fought many wars against Vijayanagara, over the Raichur Doab. He married the daughter of Devaraya I, and the rivalries ended, only to resume under later rulers. The Bahmani sultanate, strong in the time of the wazir Mahmud Gawan, also weakened as nobles of other factions conspired to kill him. It was the beginning of the end for the sultanate.

Deccan Sultanates

IMAD SHAHIS

Berar, a province of the Bahmani Sultanate, came into being in 1490 when a former governor of Berar, then based in the city of Gawil, Fathullah Imad-ul-Mulk (r. 1490–1504 CE), declared his independence. A small province in north Deccan, Berar remained an independent sultanate for only a century (1490–1574 CE). Its bigger neighbours to the south, like Ahmednagar, always eyed it.

In his small kingdom, Darya Imad Shah (r. 1530–62 CE) tried to rule with stability. He married his daughter to the Ahmednagar sultan, and came to Ahmednagar's aid during the latter's battle with Aliya Rama Raya in 1563. He also founded the city of Daryapur. But the Imad Shahis were finally overwhelmed by the more powerful state of Ahmednagar.

BARID SHAHIS

Bidar was formed over an area in present-day south-eastern Maharashtra and north-eastern Karnataka. It was founded by Qasim Barid, a slave. He rose to become prime minister to the Bahmani sultan, who by 1492 had become very weak. Both Qasim Barid and his son Amir Barid effectively controlled the Bahmani Sultanate.

Ali Barid Shah I was the first to declare himself independent in 1542. He joined the Deccan sultanates in the fight against

Vijayanagara in 1565. In 1619, Ibrahim Adil Shah of Bijapur defeated the Bidar sultan, Amir Barid.

They made extensive renovations to the fort of Bidar, one of the strongest and well-planned forts of medieval India. Bidar's craftsmen – patronized by the Bahmanis and the later Barid Shahi sultans – were known for their elaborate work with metal, called 'Bidri'.

NIZAM SHAHIS

The Ahmednagar kingdom (1490–1633 CE) lay between Gujarat in the north and Bijapur to its south. In 1490, Malik Ahmed Nizam Shah I (r. 1490–1510 CE) defeated the Bahmani general and formed an independent state. Its first capital was Junnar (later called Shivneri, a fort Shivaji would claim) and then Ahmednagar, a city in present-day Maharashtra.

Succession issues beset Ahmednagar after the death of Hussain Shah in 1565. His son Murtaza Shah was young, and it was his father's aunt Chand Bibi (who had married into the Bijapur royal family) who held power. After Murtaza's death, his son Minar Hussain ruled for a short while. He was poisoned and his cousin assumed power. In this tussle, the Mughals under Akbar intervened. A noble held power in place of Ismail Hussain, Minar's cousin, who assumed power for a while. It was Ismail's father, Burhan Nizam, who actually ruled. Chand Bibi managed to gain power and led the forces against Akbar's sons.

After Chand Bibi's death, a section of Ahmednagar's nobles led by Malik Ambar continued to resist the Mughals. Later, Shahji Bhonsle accepted service under Ahmednagar and propped up a claimant to the throne to effectively oppose Bijapur and the Mughals. He tried his best to keep alive an infant son of the Nizam Shahi dynasty at a time when Shah Jahan was hell bent on destroying the dynasty. When the young son was kidnapped, Shahji compromised. He begged the Mughals not to kill the boy, and agreed to move south as a condition. Ahmednagar finally became part of the Mughal Empire under Shah Jahan in 1633.

SOUTH INDIA

Deccan Sultanates

ADIL SHAHIS

The sultanate of Bijapur was formed about the same time as the breakup of the Bahmani empire around 1489. It resisted the Mughal advance for a long time. Bijapur was centred around western Karnataka, in present-day Bijapur district.

Ibrahim Adil Shah II was its greatest ruler (r. 1579–1626). His empire extended southward, and he was known for his appreciation of the arts. Bijapur's cosmopolitanism of the time is still reflected in its buildings.

He lost his father (Ali Adil Shah) when he was very young and the throne became a point of contention between his aunt, Chand Bibi, who was a princess of Ahmednagar as well, and ambitious nobles. Chand Bibi excelled in political machinations and young Ibrahim had as many as five regents before he became king. The brave Chand Bibi was also regent of Ahmednagar (for her nephew Bahadur Shah) and held out against the Mughal emperor Akbar's forces for a long time.

Ibrahim Adil Shah loved music and literature. He composed hymns to Saraswati in his book *Kitab-i-Navras*. He loved playing the tanpura, and named his tanpura 'Motikhan'.

In the reign of the later Bijapur sultans, Shivaji emerged as a powerful force, especially after he killed the Bijapur general Afzal Khan. Aurangzeb finally captured Bijapur in 1686.

QUTB SHAHIS

The Qutb Shahis (1518–1687 CE) of Golconda ruled over parts of present-day Andhra Pradesh and Telangana. They are known for beautiful buildings such as the Char Minar of Hyderabad and the Golconda Fort. They were patrons of not just Persian but also Telugu, and several of the rulers could use both languages with ease.

Ibrahim Quli Qutb Shah (r. 1550–80 CE) escaped an ambitious older brother and lived in Vijayanagara for seven years as a guest of Aliya Rama Raya, whom he later betrayed by ganging up with the other sultanate states to fight Vijayanagara in 1565 and destroy its fabled might.

Muhammad Quli Qutb Shah (r. 1580–1611 CE) encouraged a policy of tolerance between different communities.

VIJAYANAGARA

As many as four important dynasties constituted the Vijayanagara kingdom (1336–1646 CE). The Sangama dynasty (1336–1485 CE) was followed by the Suluvas, and the Tuluvas. A sub–branch, the Aravidus, came to dominate the Thanjavur region in the south after Vijayanagara's defeat in 1565 at the Battle of Talikota.

Founded by two brothers, Harihara and Bukka, who had earlier been imprisoned by Muhammad bin Tughlaq, the kings of Vijayanagara set new standards in cultural achievement. But the kingdom was gradually divided into different factions as areas were parcelled off among male descendants. This led to civil war in a generation or two. Their external wars were mainly with the Bahmanis for control of the Raichur Doab. Deva Raya I (r. 1406–22 CE) and Deva Raya II (r. 1424–46 CE) were powerful rulers who controlled the Kalinga region and even extended Vijayanagara's sway into Ceylon (Sri Lanka).

When capable generals assumed power, the Suluvas and Tuluvas emerged as Vijayanagara's rulers. Krishnadevaraya (r. 1509–30) of the latter dynasty was one of the greatest kings. He successfully fought against the Deccani states, and his court encouraged literature in various languages. Hampi became one of the most wonder-evoking cities of the world.

1526 Onwards

◇ NORTH INDIA ◇

MUGHALS

The Mughals (1526–1857 CE) had style, ambition and vision. For nearly 200 years, they dominated political and cultural life on the Indian subcontinent. Babur distinguished himself as a warrior and writer, his son Humayun lost the throne and recovered it, and Akbar ranked high as a king because of some of his enlightened views and policies. He showed firmness towards enemies and friendship towards allies, such as the Rajputs.

In Jahangir and Shah Jahan's time, the empire scaled fine aesthetic heights. The later Mughals, beginning with Aurangzeb, faced several challenges, including that of keeping centralized control over a large empire, which broke up in a matter of decades under Aurangzeb's successors. For all the tragedy of the later Mughals, they still retained symbolic credibility, and the warriors of 1857 marched to Delhi and declared Bahadur Shah Zafar India's emperor. After the 1857 uprising was crushed, Bahadur Shah Zafar's sons were executed by the British and he, the last Mughal emperor, was exiled to Rangoon, where he died a lonely death in 1862.

SURS/SURIS

This was a short-lived dynasty (1530–56 CE) that left its mark in history, mainly due to its visionary ruler, Sher Shah (r. 1538–45

CE). He was a canny military leader as his successive victories over Humayun showed. His financial measures, his stipulation on the rupee and his reorganization of the administration were moves that were taken up by Akbar, the Mughal ruler. His successors were too weak and divided to stand against the Mughals.

SIKHS

Ranjit Singh ruled first as chief of Sukerchakia *misl* (1792–1801), and then Emperor of Punjab (1801–39 CE). From a young age, Ranjit Singh united the different *misls* into a powerful kingdom that posed a block to the ambitions of the Afghans to the north and the British to the south. When he died, his heirs were young. After two Anglo–Sikh Wars, the British East India Company took control of the region in 1849.

WEST INDIA

MARATHAS

The Maratha Empire that Shivaji founded lasted for at least around 150 years (1674–1818), despite the problems that plagued his successors.

Chhatrapati Shivaji Maharaj (r. 1674–80) succeeded in facing first the Deccan states of Bijapur and Ahmednagar and then the might of the Mughals. His half-brother Venkoji formed a second Maratha kingdom in the south, centred around Thanjavur in present-day Tamil Nadu.

It was during the time of his grandson, Shahu I (r. 1708–49), that the first of the Peshwas emerged. It soon became a hereditary position as Balaji Vishwanath (r. 1713–20), his son, Baji Rao (r. 1720–40), and grandson, Balaji Baji Rao, advanced upon Delhi, and dominated Hyderabad and Mysore (Mysuru). Though the defeat in the 1761 Third Battle of Panipat at the hands of Ahmad Shah Abdali was a shock, the Peshwas remained a considerable force, while generals such as the Holkars, Scindias, Gaekwads and the Bhonsles gained power.

Peshwa Baji Rao II was defeated in 1818 by the British forces. This also meant the defeat of the Maratha confederacy formed by the Bhonsles, the Holkars and the Peshwa's own army. Baji Rao II's adopted son Nana Sahib would be one of the leaders of the 1857 War of Independence.

MARATHA CONFEDERACY

The confederacy was made up of generals during the time of Peshwa rule, but as the latter declined, the generals came to rule over their own independent Maratha kingdoms. It was in the time of the later Peshwas that four generals came to the forefront – the Holkars of Indore, the Scindias of Gwalior, the Gaekwads of Baroda, and the different Bhonsle families of Satara, Nagpur, Kolhapur and Thanjavur. Though they gradually lost their power to the British, they were influential right till independence and beyond.

Malhar Rao Holkar (r. 1731–66 CE) was a famous general. The East India Company was wary of him. He kept the Mughal emperor under his influence. But the shock of the defeat at Panipat in 1761 was too much for him as well. His daughter-in-law Ahilyabai (r. 1767–95 CE) ruled over Indore firmly and with kindness, and a nephew Tukoji Rao Holkar managed the kingdom's military affairs.

The Scindias of Gwalior came to the forefront first under Ranoji Rao Shinde (r. 1731–45 CE), and then Mahadji Shinde (r. 1768–94 CE), who restored Gwalior's fortunes after the 1761 Battle of Panipat by working in tandem with the Peshwa Madhav Rao in Pune. Daulat Rao Scindia, his nephew who succeeded him in 1794, ensured domination during the continuing decline of the Peshwas.

While the Gaekwads of Baroda (1721–1947 CE) ruled as a British protectorate, Baroda was known for its reformist initiatives, especially in the time of Sayajirao III.

The four Bhonsle dynasties at Nagpur, Kolhapur, Thanjavur and Satara claimed to have descended directly from Shivaji.

SOUTH INDIA

MYSURU/MYSORE

This kingdom was founded on the decline of the Vijayanagara empire by the Wodeyars. Chikka Devaraja (r. 1645–1704) instituted petty taxes that led to a revolt, which was brutally suppressed. He kept cordial relations with Mughal Emperor Aurangzeb. At a time when the Wodeyars were weak, its generals soon became effective sultans. Under Hyder Ali (r. 1761–82 CE), and Tipu Sultan (r. 1782–99 CE), Mysore reached its greatest territorial limit. But it had to wage wars on all fronts: against the Nizam of Hyderabad, the state of Travancore, the British East India Company and the Marathas. When Tipu was decisively defeated by the British forces in 1799, the kingdom, albeit in a much truncated state, was restored to the Wodeyars. A centre for cultural excellence, especially in literature and music, under the Wodeyars, it came to be known as a reform-oriented princely state, which encouraged women's education and banned child marriage.

TRAVANCORE

The Travancore kingdom was dominant from the 1720s when Marthanda Varma (r. 1729–58) built up a powerful navy, and saw off the Dutch threat at the famous two–year long battle of Colachel in 1741. Dharma Raja (r. 1758–98), who succeeded his uncle, had several confrontations with Mysore state.

FURTHER READINGS

Want to know more about the kings and queens of India? Here are a few of the many books the author referred to, which you might like to read:

1. Basham, A.L. (2004): *The Wonder That Was India: I*, Picador India: New Delhi.
2. Chandra, Satish (2007): *A History of Medieval India*, Orient Blackswan: New Delhi.
3. Chattopadhyay, Brajadulal and Kumkum Roy (2002): *Women in Early Indian Societies*, Manohar Publishers: New Delhi.
4. Gordon, Stewart (2007): *The Marathas (1600–1818)*, Cambridge University Press: UK and New Delhi.
5. Habib, Irfan (2012-); A People's History of India in several volumes, Tulika Books: New Delhi.
6. Jha, D.N. (2005): *Early India: A Concise History*, Manohar Publishers: New Delhi.
7. Lahiri, Nayanjot (2015): *Ashoka in Ancient India*, Orient Blackswan: New Delhi.
8. Nehru, Jawaharlal (2008): *The Discovery of India*, Penguin India: New Delhi.
9. Nilakanta Sastri, K.A., with Rajan Gurukkal and R. Champakalakshmi (2009): *The Illustrated History of South India: from Prehistoric Times to the Fall of Vijayanagar*, Oxford University Press: New Delhi.
10. Rizvi, S.A. (2004): *The Wonder That Was India: II*, Picador India: New Delhi.
11. Singh, Upinder (2009): *A History of Ancient and Early Medieval India: from Stone Age to the 12th Century*, Pearson Education: New Delhi.
12. Trautmann, Thomas (2015): *Elephants and Kings*, Permanent Black: New Delhi.